BASICS

LANDSCAPE ARCHITE

01

URBAN DESIGN

ethical: aware-ness/ reflect-ion/ debate

academia

An AVA Book

Published by AVA Publishing SA
Rue des Fontenailles 16
Case Postale
1000 Lausanne 6
Switzerland
Tel: +41 786 005 109
Email: enquiries@avabooks.ch

Distributed by Thames & Hudson (ex-North America)
181a High Holborn
London WC1V 7QX
United Kingdom
Tel: +44 20 7845 5000
Fax: +44 20 7845 5055
Email: sales@thameshudson.co.uk
www.thamesandhudson.com

Distributed in the USA & Canada by:
Ingram Publisher Services Inc.
1 Ingram Blvd.
La Vergne TN 37086
USA
Tel: +1 866 400 5351
Fax: +1 800 838 1149
Email: customer.service@ingrampublisherservices.com

English Language Support Office
AVA Publishing (UK) Ltd.
Tel: +44 1903 204 455
Email: enquiries@avabooks.ch

ISBN 978-2-940411-12-2

10 9 8 7 6 5 4 3 2 1

Design: an Atelier project, www.atelier.ie
Cover image by Iwan Baan © 2009

Production by AVA Book Production Pte. Ltd., Singapore
Tel: +65 6334 8173
Fax: +65 6259 9830
Email: production@avabooks.com.sg

→
Name: The High Line

Location: New York, USA

Date: 2004–2009

**Designer: Field Operations
with Diller Scofidio + Renfro**

An abandoned elevated railway
line has been transformed into
a linear park or greenway. The
High Line stretches for over two
kilometres through Manhattan's
west side. It provides a wholly
new way of experiencing the city.

Contents

Civilisation is less a thing or an institution than it is a process. It is a drive to live together in society, in close proximity, and to gain progressive benefit from that physical association. Human settlements – villages, towns and cities – are the physical manifestation of human communities and civilisation. The work of orchestrating these environments has come to be known as 'urban design'.

Urban design is the work of shaping the three-dimensional spaces of human settlements with the intention to improve not just the beauty of a place, but to allow better interaction between people and between people and their environment. Good urban design contributes to the overall quality of life in a city. As such, it is not merely a physical design process, but a balancing of political, economic, cultural and physical factors that have an impact on a given place.

Because of the immensely broad base of knowledge, context and understanding required, urban design is always collaborative work. It is a discipline that involves a range of professions. Primary amongst these professions are landscape architects, building architects and planners. Individuals in many fields work as urban designers and this is particularly important given that each profession and discipline brings different training and knowledge, and a different set of sensibilities to an urban design team. This book, therefore, seeks to explain the significance of landscape architecture to urban design and the significance of urban design to landscape architects.

→
Name: Bryant Park

Location: New York, USA

Date: 1986–1991

Designer: Laurie Olin

A crowd fills New York's Bryant Park for a special event. Urban design creates spaces for people, from individual interaction to busy festivals.

'A shared understanding of how cities now function, of the essentially democratic nature of urban public space, of an urban landscape aesthetic that is also an ecological and ethical system, is badly needed today.' Ken Worpole

Landscape architecture in urban design

Landscape architecture is a profession that combines art and science to shape and manage the physical world and the systems that we are part of. It is a design profession that creatively responds to the challenges of man's interaction with the land to propose new possibilities for sites. Landscape architecture also requires a strong understanding of natural systems and sciences, such as geology and soils, plants and climatic and water systems.

The broad, contextual knowledge of ecological systems is one of the key strengths that landscape architects bring to the work of urban design. Cities are, in one sense, simply physical manifestations of human ecology. They are human habitat and as such, at a fundamental level, they function like any other animal habitat, providing shelter, protection, refuge, and the mutual advantage of strength in numbers. Far from being merely collections of buildings, cities are interconnected, interdependent systems of movement and interaction, which require of the designer the ability to see the big picture, the confidence to act in a complex milieu, and the humility to watch, listen and learn.

Urban design in landscape architecture

Landscape architects are often called upon to lead projects in urban design, given that their training gives them exceptional context and sensitivity. Many landscape architecture firms base their practice almost entirely around urban design, not only because of the specific range of skills within the firm, but simply because such a large number of projects fall within an urban context. When considering the design of a city park, for example, it is not possible to conceive of a park as separate from its surroundings. The pathways taken by pedestrians through a town to reach the park, the enclosure of the park by buildings, the movement of vehicles and services, and the political motivations for any changes to the space are all urban design considerations that fall within the work of landscape architecture.

What does the book explain?

· The parallels between urban design and landscape architecture

· The landscape architectural techniques and context that are important in urban design

· The urban design techniques and context that are useful to landscape architecture

· How different projects worldwide show the interconnections between urban design and landscape architecture

The global population has become increasingly more urban and concentrated over the course of the last few centuries. Urbanisation may be seen as a natural, even ecological process that, like natural wilderness, is frequently imbalanced, contentious or dangerous. Designing and planning for urban environments demands a contextual approach and an awareness of overlapping and interdependent systems in much the same way that planning for the larger environment does. Indeed, urbanisation has now impacted on so much of the larger environment that a new field called landscape urbanism has come into being.

This book explains, at least in broad terms, the relationship between the profession of landscape architecture and the practice of urban design. This would be a simple task if one was a subset of the other, or if landscape architecture and urban design were separate disciplines that undertook completely different types of work. However, there are many overlaps, similarities and complementary approaches between the two. This book attempts to give sufficient background for the reader to understand why decisions are made in urban design rather than to explain specific methods or techniques.

↑

Name: Gardens by the Bay

Location: Singapore

Date: 2006

Designer: Grant Associates

This winning entry from Singapore's Gardens by the Bay competition is based upon providing substantial green infrastructure for a sustainable city. The Lion Grove features imposing 'Supertrees' that will provide shade by day and lighting by night.

The two main discussions in this book are:

· the relevance of landscape architecture to urban design and

· the relevance of urban design to landscape architecture.

There are six chapters in this book, each presenting a different aspect of this discourse:

What is urban design? – This section provides an introduction to the histories, theories, design firms, and designers that have shaped our understanding of urban design. This provides a background for understanding the design and planning of cities, and the debates that surround the definition of urban design.

Context – Understanding context, whether environmental, social, or political, is fundamental to landscape architecture. Techniques for analysing context developed by landscape architects have become instrumental to the practice of urban design as well.

Measure – How big? How much? How fast? How many? The measure of the city greatly informs both our understanding of it and the emergence of new urban forms. This section discusses measure and scale from the micro detail to the macro super block, and from the local to the global.

Movement – This section highlights the development of movement systems in urban centres. The recent trends for shared space are contrasted with traditional approaches to mass transit and the emerging methodologies in contemporary metropolises.

Community and culture – Culture has a profound effect on the landscape and it is also, in turn, deeply influenced by place. Urban design processes succeed or fail depending on their acceptance by the community. Cultural and community contexts are essential to understand in order to create meaningful urban form.

Projects and processes – Many of the key themes of the book are reintroduced in this section, and the opportunity is taken to highlight particular issues using important design projects as lenses through which to view them.

→

Name: Borneo Sporenburg

Location: Amsterdam, the Netherlands

Date: 1993

Designer: West 8

The landscape architecture firm West 8 is renowned for its urban design that is both eye-catching and functional. This pedestrian bridge links the two peninsulas of this development across the canal.

Urban Design

This book introduces different aspects of urban design in landscape architecture via dedicated chapters for each topic. Each chapter provides an in-depth look at these various elements and considerations. The examples included offer a wide range of projects, and together with detailed analysis in the text, form a book that offers a unique insight into urban design.

Section headers

Each chapter is broken down into sub-sections, the title of which can be found at the top left-hand corner of each spread.

Box outs

Contain more detailed and contextual information about topics in urban design, which are discussed in the text.

City

44–45

Each city provides a unique context. As a landscape architect or urban designer it is important to identify the layers that create these environments; understanding the diagram of the city as well as the image that the city projects is essential for designers working within this context.

Political contexts

Separating the political contexts from that of the economy is a formidable task. However, some city leaders are beginning to use local urban policy to distinguish their cities in national and global contexts. These individuals and their policies offer new tools and avenues for urban design. Enrique Peñalosa, Jaime Lerner and Ken Livingstone are three former mayors who have been recognised as transforming their respective cities of Bogotá, Curitiba and London. Many urban designers have worked with these city leaders in guiding policy and city-wide projects; many more have then developed proposals for specific sites within the context of new layers of policy. In the City of London, new policies have resulted in movement systems, such as London's Congestion Charge system, and, more locally, in projects such as the redesign of Trafalgar Square.

Political contexts have also contributed to the specific urban forms of Soweto in the shadow of apartheid policy; the proposals for Berlin by Hitler's architect, Albert Speer; and the modern fantasy of Lucio Costa's Brasília. These cities are some of the most obvious examples of planning in a political context by strong and often ruthless politicians. However, as seen in Bogotá, Curitiba and London, policy-led urban design can also achieve great benefit for citizens and projects at more local scales.

The political city

The exercise of power and authority in politics often has profound implications on the spaces of the city. In particular, political decisions often result in the creation of either zones or divisions. Dramatic examples of how politics might include Amsterdam's famous red light district, which defines an urban area unto itself for the Green Line (separating the Turkish and Greek halves of Cyprus's capital, Nicosia).

More subtle but equally striking examples of the political shaping of cities might include Amsterdam's famous red light district, which defines an urban area unto itself for the business of sex workers, or the designations of office districts, such as London's Canary Wharf or Berlin's Potsdamer Platz. Each presumably keeps unsavoury occupations, such as prostitution or banking, at arm's length.

Name: Diagram of the divisions in Nicosia
Location: Cyprus
Date: n/a
Designer: n/a

Much of the divided city of Nicosia remains within its sixteenth-century Venetian fortifications. Within these walls, two contrasting political contexts – the Greek Cypriot community to the south and the Turkish Cypriot community to the north – have existed for several decades. A UN buffer zone – the Green Line – marks this line of separation of politics and people.

'Nothing is experienced by itself, but always in relation to its surroundings, the sequence of events leading up to it, the memory of past experiences.' Kevin Lynch

Context
← City and territory **City** Neighbourhoods and blocks →

Pull quotes

Tips and insights from key individuals in landscape architecture and urban design.

Captions

Supply contextual information about the images and help connect the visuals with key concepts discussed in the body text.

Chapter introductions

Provide an overview of the key concepts and ideas that the chapter will explore.

Images

Photographs and illustrations from an array of professional practices bring the text to life.

Mass vs individual

106 — 107

The futuristic dream of people gliding noiselessly through the city in individual capsules is still not a reality, nor might it ever be. Living in densely packed urban environments requires mass, usually public, transportation and alternative individual movement networks. Working out the right balance between the two increasingly requires an understanding of the multiple scales of the city, from the local to the global, and an anticipation of the fluctuating users of the space.

Individual movement

Individual movement is about choice. Choosing when to leave, which route to take and who to travel with makes individual movement systems extremely popular. The bulk of individual movement through the city is on a very local basis and is shaped by daily needs: trips to the shops and post office, exercising pets and taking children to school. In many countries, these individual journeys are made primarily on foot, though there has been, both in the developed and developing worlds, an inexorable trend towards the design of cities where the car is a necessity. Once a utopian dream advocated by architects such as Le Corbusier, many of the modernist planning projects, which only decades ago prioritised the car above the pedestrian, are being demolished and rebuilt for a pedestrian future.

While mass transport has its fixed routes and times, alternative means of travel, such as walking, cycling, or driving, usually convey the individual directly from their point of departure to their destination. They all provide door-to-door service.

It is important for urban designers to test their designs with many of these journeys as a way of refining their projects and understanding the implications.

→ ↗
Name: Bicycle Flat – images and cross-sections
Location: Amsterdam, the Netherlands
Date: 2001
Designer: VMX Architects

High population density and the overwhelming popularity of the bicycle as a mode of individual transport in Amsterdam created the need for this enormous bicycle parking garage at Central Station. It was built as a temporary structure to accommodate bicycle parking during renovations, but it may serve as a model for a more sustainable future.

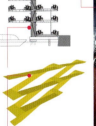

Movement
← Modes **Mass vs individual** Stasis →

Navigation guides

Help the reader to determine which chapter unit they are in and what the preceding and following sections are.

Diagrams

Help to explain landscape architectural theory and concepts in more detail.

Urban design is a practice that is at once young and old. People have consciously shaped the landscapes in which they live for millennia. This includes the settlements that form a major part of that landscape. These settlements provide frameworks for human existence. As a distinct discipline, urban design dates to the middle of the twentieth century. It exists at the intersection of architecture, landscape architecture, and landscape and urban planning.

This young field is still being defined. It may, in fact, be impossible to define its boundaries, as its subjects – towns and cities – are constantly changing. What we can agree, though, is that urban design is a creative, collaborative process that involves shaping the forms of the city, enhancing the experience of it, and improving its function as a habitat for human life.

←
....

Name: East Jerusalem Master Plan

Location: Jerusalem, Israel

Date: 1999

Designer: Sorkin Studio

This plan is a schematic proposal. It begins by suggesting that the political and commercial sprawl of the city be halted and that further development be a thickening of existing built-up territory. It further suggests that the Kidron River Valley to the east of the old city of Jerusalem be re-naturalised to become a central green space. The aim is to serve both east and west Jerusalem, and to secure the future of this historically and culturally charged space.

Urban design is a broad field that does not sit within one profession. Its range and meaning is a source of debate, and the following section sheds light on this ever-changing discipline.

Definitions across the architectures

The emergence of urban design as a modern discipline can possibly be traced to a conference held at the Graduate School of Design at Harvard University in the United States, held at the behest of the School's then Dean, José Lluís Sert, also an accomplished city planner. The conference's stated goal was as follows: 'This Invitation Conference is intended to be exploratory, not didactic, and to try and find a common basis for the joint work of the Architect, the Landscape Architect and the City Planner in the field of Urban Design.'[1]

Many at the conference were justifiably concerned that city planning had become a sterile, scientific profession that was 'mainly occupied with a quick return on investment' rather than with the real needs of people within their built environment – community and individual needs that included not just firmness and commodity, but beauty and delight.

In their introduction to the *Urban Design Reader*, Matthew Carmona and Steve Tiesdell state that 'there are (very) few "hard-and-fast" rules or absolutes in urban design – substantially because the process of design involves relating general (and generally desirable) principles to site and programme requirements, where the context and creative vision will always vary.'[2] In other words, urban design can never be formulaic, as the response to every place will always be both specific and unique. As such, a 'scientific' approach is neither desirable nor is it even possible.

While it may not be possible to create formulas, there are still political and ideological motivators that may inform designs differently. Today, for example, a struggle continues between those who couch discussions of urban quality in real estate terms; those who have come to realise that urban design focused on boosting profits can actually provide a quick return on investment; and those who insist that intangibles, such as community and happiness, are the real drivers. In reality, a middle ground that allows communities to flourish along with developers is likely to profit everyone most.

'...a city is a dramatic event in the environment.' Gordon Cullen

What is urban design?

There is still plenty of debate as to the scope and the goals of urban design. There is consensus, though, that the work of urban design exists at the intersection of architecture, landscape architecture and city planning, and there is also a general agreement that urban design is:

- a creative process

- a collaborative, interdisciplinary process and

- a place-making process that involves creating three-dimensional urban forms and space, which enhance the experience of towns and cities.

What is an urban designer?

A central debate in urban design is whether the term 'urban designer' has any real meaning. If there is such a discipline as urban design, then it follows that one who practises within the discipline should be called an urban designer. Indeed, there are a number of university programmes that prepare students for exactly this role. The problem, though, is in the vastness of the field. The question: 'But what do you do?' might still remain. It is necessary to identify within what area of the field one is a practitioner.

Further, there are no professional bodies that provide legal definitions, university accreditation, organised testing for qualifications, or insurance for urban design as a profession. For the time being, it is still necessary for an individual practitioner to qualify within one of the architectural or planning professions in order to provide the assurance of adequate legal and financial protection, and stringent professional and ethical standards. This professional standing can then be the ideal platform for specialisation in urban design.

1. *Progressive Architecture* (1956), vol. XXXVII, no. 8 (August): p. 97, quoted in Gosling, David, *The Evolution of American Urban Design*, Chichester, Wiley-Academy, 2003. p. 34.

2. Carmona, Matthew and Tiesdell, Stephen. *Urban Design Reader*. Oxford and Burlington, MA, Architectural Press, 2007. p. 1.

Future directions

There are many potential directions for the future of urban design, and there are even some historical utopian models that may yet be realised. However, one of the most significant developments in urban design over the last 20 years is the emergence of the field of landscape urbanism. This heralds a fundamental shift in the understanding of urban settlements. Charles Waldheim proclaims that 'landscape urbanism describes a disciplinary realignment currently underway in which landscape replaces architecture as the basic building block of contemporary urbanism'.[1] It is now becoming globally recognised that sustainable urbanism must look to context – the landscape – rather than buildings alone for solutions. The profound implication is that landscape architecture and planning must emerge as the professions that will lead the way into the future, carrying the banner of holistic environmental design.

The process of re-imagining the possibilities for urbanism proposed by a landscape-centred thinking is built on the work of generations of ecologists, artists, theorists, and designers, who, like the landscape architect Ian McHarg, recognised the symbiotic relationship between humans and their habitat. Urban designers must continue to respond to changing urban patterns, whether this is the accelerating informal settlements of the global South cities, or the result of decades of suburban sprawl in the global North. The decades ahead will be crucial to balancing human needs with the survival of the planet as we know it, and landscape architects have the potential to lead the way in the field of urban design.

↘ →
....

Name: Sun City, Mumbai slums and Dongtan Eco-city

Location: USA, India and China

Date: Various

Designer: Various

What does the future hold for our cities? Visions range from the utopian to the apocalyptic, but the reality will probably be somewhere in between. Landscape architects engaged in urban design will play an ever-increasing role in deciding this future. Pictured are (top to bottom): the cultural monotony of Sun City in Arizona, USA; the sprawling slums of Mumbai, India; and the optimistic vision for Dongtan Eco-city in China.

1. Waldheim, Charles, (ed). *The Landscape Urbanism Reader*. Princeton Architectural Press, New York, 2006. p. 11.

Cities are mankind's greatest built works, but they are also habitat for an impressively wide range of species and highly complex ecosystems. Cities have evolved just as individual species have, and this section offers a brief thumbnail sketch of this process.

From the rural to the urban

Some 10,000 years ago, humans began to cultivate the earth instead of hunting and gathering. The first settlements were small, but the interdependent relationship between towns and the surrounding countryside was established. Food supply, transport, security, shelter and community remain the primary reasons for humans to live together in urban settlements. These needs shaped the way we used and built the landscape both inside and outside of settlements. People who live together make decisions together on how they build and shape their communities. These decisions, whether formal or informal, would have formed rudimentary urban planning.

Cities and the countryside evolved together through the millennia. The landscape architect Geoffrey Jellicoe, in his seminal book *The Landscape of Man*, separates the evolution of cities through their civilisations: Central civilisations, Eastern civilisations, Western civilisations, and Modern civilisations beginning from the eighteenth century.[1] This allows the reader to picture the development of cities and landscapes, such as Beijing, Kyoto, Luxor, Athens, Paris and London. On the other hand, presenting these developments in parallel may show an inevitable forward thrust we might call progress.

It is more useful to view development as responding to changing needs and circumstances; similar patterns occurred at different times everywhere in the world. Spiro Kostof's great studies of human settlements, *The City Shaped* and *The City Assembled* analyse cities through patterns and meanings showing how these evolved into form.[2] These books show that forms are invested and suffused with human meaning, history and movement.

1. Jellicoe, Geoffrey and Susan. *The Landscape of Man: Shaping the Environment from Prehistory to the Present Day*, Thames and Hudson, 1995.

2. Kostof, Spiro. *The City Shaped: Urban Patterns and Meanings Through History*. Thames and Hudson, 1999. And Kostof, Spiro. *The City Assembled: The Elements of Urban Form Through History*. Thames and Hudson, 1999.

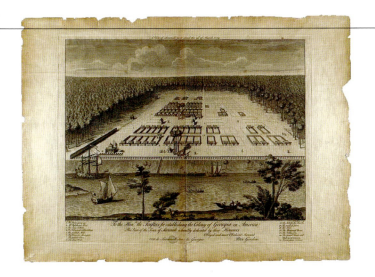

←

Name: Savannah

Location: Savannah, USA

Date: c1733

Designer: James Oglethorpe

Savannah was based on an egalitarian grid and remains a progressive model for urban planning.

↘ →

Name: New Lanark

Location: Scotland, UK

Date: c1800

Designer: Robert Owen

New Lanark was a town operated on socialist and cooperative principles by the reformer Robert Owen. Owen was a pioneer in childcare reform and treated workers well. The beautiful and salubrious setting of the mill is a physical reflection of his principles.

The growth of the city

The very earliest human settlements were little more than clusters of dwellings, but even then the basic forms that we live in today were already established. Houses were arranged around a hearth and there were defined areas for living, working and sleeping. These settlements often had streets that linked the dwellings, and there were also areas for disposing of household rubbish. Transporting food and goods, handling waste, and providing places for meeting and exchanging ideas are common to all human settlements everywhere and throughout civilisation. Most settlements grew in places favoured by geography, such as river crossings or fords, sheltered valleys, crossroads and natural harbours.

However, these patterns are deceptively peaceful. Urban history and form show us that humans have been covetous, vengeful and bloodthirsty through the ages, just as much as they have been quiet and productive. City walls and fortresses were facts of life in most parts of the world as people tried to protect what they had gained, and also provide a fortified base from which to issue forth to grab more.

A city's walls could not always contain all its inhabitants or commerce for long. Many times, cities would build successive rings of walls to contain growth as they spread ever outward. Sprawl is anything but a new pattern. Even the earliest civilisations in Mesopotamia would have known it.

In the industrial age, cities grew explosively, bursting from behind the medieval walls and stretching out across the countryside. Many of our contemporary urban issues stem from this massive growth and the vehicles that have evolved to serve it – from the steam train to the tram to the automobile. New urban forms, such as the strip (linear, usually commercial development along road corridors) and the edge city (self-contained ex- or suburban settlements often comprising private office and commercial development), require completely new ways of thinking and acting.

Most recently, issues of international migration rather than migration from the countryside have informed the way that many Western cities grow. Due to the accelerating growth of urban informal settlements, the United Nations (the UN Habitat, in particular) have invested in projects and policies to manage this growth and improve the quality of life of those migrating to and between cities. It is important to recognise the potentials of this new urban growth with the hope that 'by including international migrants as an integral part [of the city]'[1], urban designers can promote new models for the design of the contemporary city.

1. Balbo, Marcello, (ed). *International Migrants and the City.* UN Habitat 2005.

↓ →

Name: Mexico City

Location: Mexico City, Mexico

Date: n/a

Designer: n/a

The map of Mexico City (right) before the conquest shows the city in the midst of a lake, much like the lagoon city of Venice. Cities grow, but often the language of the place is indelible. The pyramids at Teotihuacan (below bottom) are recalled, as is the city in the lake, in the pond at the Conjunto Juárez (below).

Cities first developed in the Fertile Crescent of the Levant and Mesopotamia and the foundations of these first cities often still exist, as at the legendary Ziggurat of Ur. The forms of cities have changed since then, but many of the functions remain the same.

Ancient

The history of great cities has tended to coincide with written language. Therefore, some records of the very earliest attempts at urban design exist. The great conquerors and rulers tend to be associated with urban visions, and not necessarily those proto-designers and bureaucrats who would have been involved in the nitty-gritty work. The earliest cities, such as the seat of Sumerian power at Ur, had an apparently organic cellular structure with only a few streets serving networks of courtyard-centred dwellings. Archaeological excavations at Çatalhöyük in Turkey have shown a similar arrangement. Though active design is evident in many of the earliest settlements, the names of those who shaped these landscapes are lost to us.

It was not until Ancient Greece that the 'father of urban planning' – Hippodamus of Miletus – would emerge. He is often credited with the invention of the modular grid in urban planning. Only the city of Miletus in Ionia has been directly attributed to him. The grid is an expression both of human dominion over the landscape and reflective of divine order. Alexander the Great's planner and architect, Dinocrates, certainly eclipses Hippodamus. Dinocrates planned the city of Alexandria and was the architect of numerous temples.

The Greek gridded town plans, which, under the reign of Alexander became distributed throughout the empire, eventually reached a form of perfection under the Romans. Again, the grid was part of the language of conquest and empire, and the formal lines of the outposts of the Roman Empire were a reminder not merely of their dominion over nature, but over their imperial subjects.

→
....
Name: The Neolithic city of Çatalhöyük

Location: Çatalhöyük, Turkey

Date: c7000 BCE

Designer: n/a

The Neolithic city of Çatalhöyük was a dense cluster of dwellings that shared walls and were accessed through openings in the roofs. Çatalhöyük is one of the largest and earliest Neolithic sites ever discovered.

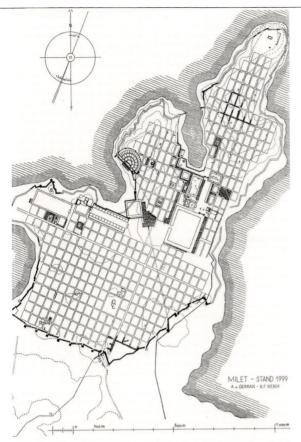

MILET - STAND 1999
A. v. GERKAN - B.F. WEBER

←

Name: Miletus

Location: Ionia, now Turkey

Date: Fifth century BCE

Designer: Hippodamus of Miletus

The plan for Miletus shows that the grid, while efficient, requires a certain genius in adapting to topography.

Leaving the medieval

Cities through the Middle Ages are often assumed to have grown 'organically', arising naturally and spontaneously upon sites favoured by geography. This is only true to a certain extent. The siting of cities has always depended upon the availability of food, water and other resources, such as transportation and the need for defence. All these conscious choices immediately militate against the idea of 'unplanned' development. Certainly, there are striking examples of cities that have taken advantage of landforms to great effect, such as at Edinburgh where the Royal Mile climbs up a glacial landscape. The French city of Carcassonne occupies and fortifies a similar outcropping. Both cities have been sites of occupation for millennia, and both were of strategic interest to the Romans.

Aside from the need to create bold ramparts and battlements for defence, one of the primary drivers for urban growth over time has been trade. Great mercantile cities, such as Bruges and Florence, were founded on the trade of textiles; the great wealth they brought was reflected in the gracious dwellings to be found in both towns. Social and political order and control were both exercised in and by cities, and this control could take the form of either monarchic power or of the church, or, in many cases, both. Esfahan in Persia was a seat of both earthly and secular power under Shah Abbas. Interestingly, Esfahan is and was notable for its sprawling bazaar as well – a teeming conglomeration of mosques, suqs, hammams and caravanserais, and of which Spiro Kostof writes: 'These non-residential business premises...were in reality total social entities – which makes a telling contrast to our own shopping malls, where by and large you only shop and eat.'[1] Traditional cities everywhere show the same sort of multilayered, multivalent structure, which runs directly counter to contemporary patterns of zoned urbanism.

Name: Sforzinda

Location: Unbuilt

Date: c1464

Designer: Filarete (Antonio di Pietro Averlino)

Filarete's Sforzinda was a conceptual ideal city, the perfect geometric order of which was to reflect a perfect political and social order. This zoned settlement, far from being democratic, was expressive of the centralised power of a monarch.

Name: Neuf-Brisach

Location: Alsace, France

Date: 1699

Designer: Marquis de Vauban

The fortified town of Neuf-Brisach was built in the reign of Louis XIV to defend the French border in the disputed region of Alsace. Unlike Sforzinda, its plan was purely defensive, and the gridded order of its streets was designed for military efficiency.

1. Kostof, Spiro. *The City Assembled: The Elements of Urban Form Through History.* Thames and Hudson, 1999. p. 99.

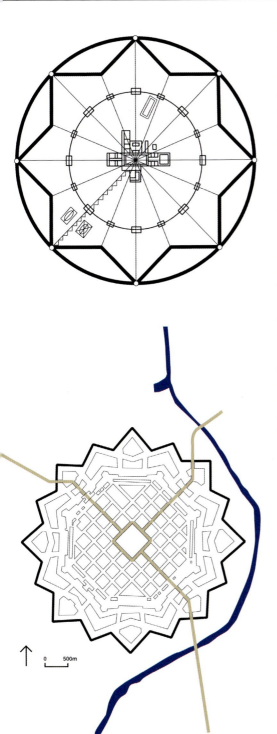

Approaching the Renaissance

Urban zoning, the process of separating urban areas according to discrete land uses, is not a new concept and may well date back to the gridded towns developed by the Greeks and Romans. It is certainly apparent in patterns for rational, ideal cities. Filarete, an architect of the early Renaissance, planned an ideal city to be called Sforzinda, based upon the pattern of an eight-pointed star. Sforzinda was more a diagram than it was a city, with government palaces at the centre hub, and trade and transportation flowing out along the radiating avenues. Sforzinda was never built, but many towns, especially fortified ones such as Neuf Brisach in Alsace and Palmanova near Venice, were built in very similar forms. These rigidly organised and zoned communities, with regularised and regimented forms, were perfectly suited to the requirements of a garrison town.

Rationalism and humanism combined in a city that was truly the heart of the Renaissance: Florence. The great flowering of the arts and culture that occurred here at the beginning of the fifteenth century had a tremendous influence not just on architecture, but on the shaping of cities in general. The Palazzo Vecchio, for example, gains its significance and impact from its siting in the Piazza della Signoria.

The idea that great societies should be housed in great and gracious cities had its roots in Florence, and would influence some of the most significant city plans, from Mannheim in Germany to the New Town in Edinburgh, Scotland.

0   500m

The Industrial Revolution was a time of convulsive change, and during this time both the city and the larger landscape began to take on the forms we could recognise in modernity.

Building the industrial

So much has been written about the Industrial Revolution that it hardly needs to be introduced here. Smoke-filled cities, overcrowding, hunger, disease and death were the defining characteristics of urban life for tragically large numbers of people. In response to these conditions, many philanthropists and planners began to explore better models for industrial communities and the industrial city.

Of all the great designers and theorists of the industrial age, there are three reformers whose ideas stand out as among the most influential of the time: Charles Fourier, Ebenezer Howard and Robert Owen. These men shared a belief that communities could be designed to improve the lot of the common person. Although only a few of these communities were ever realised, including Owen's New Lanark and Howard's Letchworth Garden City, the influence of these utopian ideals on successive generations of architects and planners is far reaching.

Almost 50 years before the founding of the New Town of Letchworth, Ildefonso Cerdà proposed a dramatic new plan for the growing industrial city of Barcelona. Following on from early gridiron plans of the Renaissance cities, the Barcelona plan included rigidly gridded octagonal blocks, sliced across on the diagonal by two grand boulevards, one of which is appropriately called the 'Avinguda (Avenue) Diagonal'. Cerdà's giant blocks have become synonymous with the concept of the gridiron plan and remain in stark contrast to the old medieval Barri Gòtic, which appears as a nugget of a tightly grained city, engulfed by the larger grid.

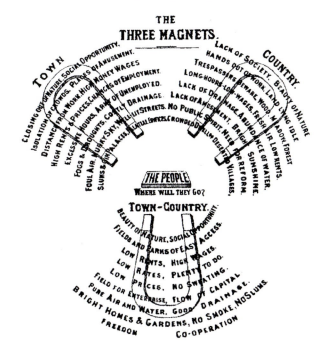

THE THREE MAGNETS.

←

Name: Three Magnets Diagram

Location: n/a

Date: 1898

Designer: Ebenezer Howard

The ideal garden city provides all the benefits of both town and country and few, if any, of their drawbacks. Howard's famous diagram from his book, *Garden Cities of Tomorrow*, illustrates the choices people might make between three compelling options – 'Town', 'Country' or 'Town-Country' – the best, of course, being 'Town-Country'.

→

Name: Saltaire

Location: Bradford, UK

Date: 1853

Designer: Sir Titus Salt

The industrialist and social reformer Sir Titus Salt built the model town of Saltaire with the needs of his workers in mind. Most of the working class at the time would have been housed in slums, but Salt's paternalistic philanthropy provided for body and mind in a healthful environment.

Greening the industrial

While Cerdà was perfecting the grid plan in Barcelona, the United States was looking to Europe for ideas on how to make spaces in the city, to provide an escape from the industrial hubbub. After visiting Birkenhead Park in Liverpool, England, in 1850, a young Fredrick Law Olmsted returned to New York with inspiration that would form his ideas for some of the greatest urban parks ever built. Olmsted's urbanism was more in keeping with what we would call 'green infrastructure' today. His parks, such as Central Park in New York and particularly his 'Emerald Necklace' network of parks in Boston, were built as both human spaces for recreation and as ecological systems that worked to control flooding and provide habitat.

The industrial age was to see advances in many aspects of urban life. It was a time of great urban growth: from the canals of Manchester in England to the department stores of Chicago in the United States, new models for new ways of living were thrust into the landscape. These advances generated notable successes, as well as failures, which would provide a basis for the founding of the modern city in the twentieth century.

↑

Name: Birkenhead Park

Location: Liverpool, UK

Date: 1847

Designer: Joseph Paxton

Frederick Law Olmsted was inspired to design Central Park after a visit to Paxton's Birkenhead Park. It broke new ground as the first publicly funded city park in Britain.

→

Name: Central Park

Location: New York, USA

Date: 1857–1873

Designer: Frederick Law Olmsted and Calvert Vaux

Central Park is one of the world's greatest parks, not just for its meaning and value to New Yorkers, but for its symbolic value as a grand, publicly minded gesture. It is an integral and vital part of the fabric of the city.

Convulsive change throughout the twentieth century radically restructured, for better or worse, all aspects of life – from society and culture to the built environment. Modernism was the prevailing style in city centres, but a mix of historicist styles held sway in the explosive growth of suburbia.

Modern cities

Modernism began with the assumption that it could completely reshape cities in bold new forms. Many modernists proposed a complete rejection of traditional styles, assuming the landscape as a tabula rasa onto which new architectural forms could be arranged and exhibited. The architecture critic, Jonathan Glancey, describes modernism as a 'moral force and a philosophical investigation' that due to its many disciples and contradictions appeared more 'like a religion'.[1] In the context of landscape architecture, the modern movement began slowly; landscape architects embraced the modern aesthetic over the aspiration that 'form follows function'. Most importantly, most modernist landscape architects focused their proposals on the ideal of the Californian garden, simultaneously rejecting the scale of the city and accepting modern landscape as an aesthetic stage on which modern buildings could perform.

The design of the modern city became the activity of the city planner. While architects such as Le Corbusier, Mies Van Der Rohe and Frank Lloyd Wright speculated visions of the modern city – the notable examples of built modern cities are the primary work of planners. Frank Lloyd Wright's Broadacre City, and Le Corbusier's Ville Contemporaine, Ville Radieuse and Plan Voisin remained unrealised utopias. However, their influence was to set the direction for future designs of the city. Founded by Le Corbusier in 1929, the Congrès International d'Architecture Moderne (CIAM) promoted many of the ideas developed by these visionary architects. In the years to follow, particularly after the Second World War, CIAM's ideals greatly influenced new cities around the globe, such as Lucio Costa's plans for Brasilia and the reconstruction of old cities, such as war-damaged Rotterdam.

1. Glancey, Jonathan. *20th Century Architecture.* Carlton Books. 2000. p. 124.

↑ ↓ →
....
Name: The postwar transformation of Rotterdam

Location: Rotterdam, Netherlands

Date: n/a

Designer: n/a

The Dutch city of Rotterdam was razed to the ground by Nazi forces early in The Second World War. Much of the city was then rebuilt on altruistic modernist principles, providing spacious housing with plenty of access to light and air.

After the modern

Modern cities broke further from traditional urban forms than the aestheticised modern architecture. The new cities were built around the automobile and the modern metropolis was emerging as a horizontal landscape of superblocks and shopping malls, serviced by wide highways and fields of asphalt parking lots. This new way of living, built by urban planners such as Robert Moses, was soon to attract strong critics. These large public projects were seen to destroy all that got in their way; by the late 1950s, a movement to recognise the qualities of local communities, traditions and landscapes began to emerge with force. In opposition to Moses' vast infrastructure projects, Jane Jacobs published the seminal book *The Death and Life of Great American Cities,* marking a new appreciation for city life and a new perspective for urban design. The reactions against these modern projects were as diverse as the modern movement itself and although modernism often projected itself as a rupture with the past, many ideas were borrowed from before and even more permeated into future generations. Decades after Jacobs faced up to Moses' plans for the Lower Manhattan Expressway in order to save her West Village neighbourhood, traces of modernist ideals can be seen developed, combined and adapted to promote both the idea of the city and the lives of its inhabitants.

→
Name: Strøget

Location: Copenhagen, Denmark

Date: 1962

Designer: Gehl Architects

An early, highly successful and influential example of an urban car-free zone was created on Copenhagen's lengthy shopping street, the Strøget. Pedestrianisation has often been effective in creating quality public streets, but, if ill-designed, it can serve to actually decrease business and occupation.

→

Name: Fresh Kills Lifescape

Location: Staten Island, USA

Date: Ongoing

Designer: Field Operations

The adaptive reuse of urban wasteland, often called 'brownfield' land, is fundamental to the designs for Fresh Kills.

←

Name: Pavilion for Hanover Expo 2000

Location: Hanover, Germany

Date: 2000

Designer: MVRDV

Innovation for sustainability created a bold and inspiring building at the 2000 Expo in Hanover, containing working plantings and using renewable technologies. Landscape architects see the whole city as a working landscape and this approach, combined with visionary architecture, can begin to answer many of the pressing problems of our day.

What is urban design?

The now and future city

While urban design has been establishing itself as a new practice for the design of cities, the theoretical speculations of future cities have also continued. In the last 50 years, modern projects have continued to be dreamt and imagined. The Barbican Centre, built by the Greater London Council, and the founding of Team 10 are clear examples of the CIAM legacy. Archigram and Superstudio stole from the public imagination, borrowing images from pop art and technology from engineering. Urban theorists looked to the environment and ecology for answers.

Artists and activists began to recognise the inherent values of the landscape. Robert Smithson's art and writing projects of the 1960s described context and time in the environment, while Ian McHarg's approach to planning was led by the analysis of natural systems. These approaches, developed by McHarg, Smithson and many of their contemporaries, were influenced by biologists, such as Sir Patrick Geddes, in order to propose new projects that would work with the landscape. Now, in the early twenty-first century, the importance of this pioneering environmental work is widely accepted. Landscape urbanism is indebted to this history, as are our aspirations for a global sustainable future.

While projects advocating social sustainability are proposing new zero carbon cities, in spite of the remediating efforts of landscape urbanism projects, these concepts remain exceptions to urban design. The dark side of contemporary urban design remains dominated by neo-liberal economics that put economic development before social and environmental concerns. Slum cities, segregation and environmental inequality are still sadly and increasingly present in this generation. The future city must wean itself off urban blocks that are scaled to car-parking ratios, avoid buildings that represent the combined egos of the client and the architect, and not sell public space as a tool for gentrification. Instead, the city can imagine new models for movement, dream buildings that are the aspirations of its people, and open up parks that are the pride of the city and all those who live in it.

↑

Name: Burj Dubai

Location: Dubai, United Arab Emirates

Date: Completion 2009

Designer: Skidmore, Owings and Merrill

Whether skyscrapers are part of a sustainable model for urban growth remains a matter of hot dispute. While high-density projects offer many benefits, such intensely concentrated land use can be immensely difficult and resource-intensive to operate and maintain.

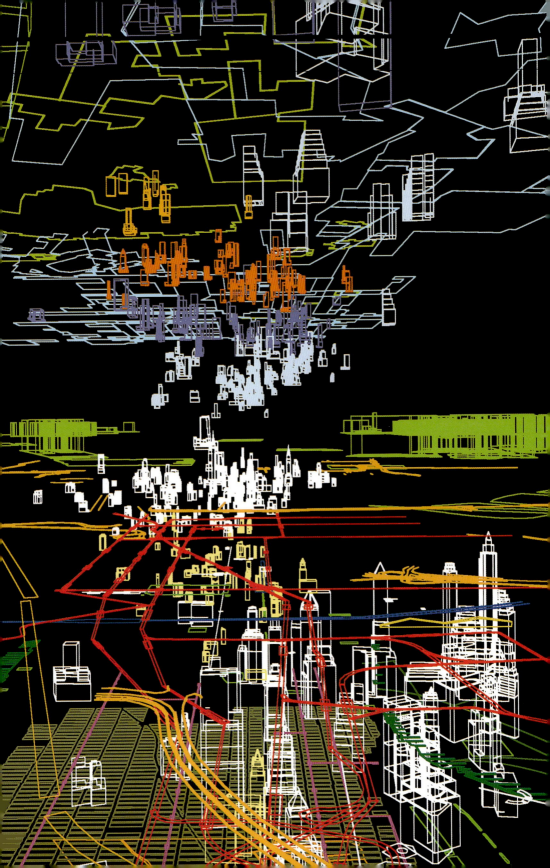

Urban contexts are about relationships. The legibility of these often complex relationships allows us in turn to make sense of the city. As inhabitants of the city, we learn to read interactions between adjacent urban areas, spaces and objects. However, as urban designers, we must also be able to understand the context for new proposals and anticipate the new relationships that will be created by our designs.

Contexts are evident from the scale of the urban territory to the scale of the material detail. Macro-scale issues, such as where a new city is sited and its distance from neighbouring cities, were crucial considerations for Peter the Great when in 1712 he announced plans for St Petersburg – a new capital city on the banks of the Neva river. In Barcelona, we can see new neighbourhood areas, such as Diagonal Mar, simultaneously responding to the historical context of the Cerda city plan and the geographic context of the seafront.

Landscape architecture responds to contexts at multiple scales and from diverse perspectives, and this responsiveness can be equally applied to urban design. All cities should be uniquely embedded in the context of their territory; neighbourhoods should be both integrated and distinct, while designed open spaces should recognise context within the multiple scales of the city.

←
....
Name: Manhattan Timeformations

Location: Manhattan, New York, USA

Date: 2001

Designer: Brian McGrath

This research project for the Skyscraper Museum mapped Manhattan's skyscraper district through time. The interactive animation on the website shows dynamic layered urban information that provides a context for existing and future projects in the city.

The territory of the city was once only described as the land immediately surrounding a settlement. Farmland, woodland and material resources from the territory historically supplied the city to sustain its population. As global networks have become more pervasive, contemporary cities have developed complex territories that transcend the physical landscape.

Geographical context

Cities are usually established in favourable territory. Considerations such as defensive positions, trading, movement of resources and the environment have had an impact on the design of new settlement.

The defensive position for territories has been a consistent factor in the positioning of cities in the landscape. For example, the walled city of Bruges has successive layers of fortifications that can be traced back to a settlement built in the first century to protect the coastline from pirates.

The emergence of global mercantile cities (such as Hong Kong, Singapore, Liverpool and Hamburg) in the eighteenth century were due less to defensive positions than to global trade routes, sheltered harbours, proximity to population centres and hospitable governments. In the twenty-first century, a new generation of port cities succeed due to their deep and wide ports, and access to a network of secondary port cities. The port of Rotterdam is a good example, having extended its port out towards the North Sea to accommodate the ever-larger supertankers, while benefitting from its central location within a growing European network.

Mineral cities are classic boom towns, such as those created by the famous gold rushes of the nineteenth century. Little consideration is given to any context except to that of the most valuable resource. Once resources are depleted, settlements are abandoned. Despite this trend, there are still several surviving mineral cities, such as South Africa's Johannesburg.

The context for old cities and the siting of new settlements is constantly changing. Understanding these contexts allows designers a perspective on how the city should be laid out and how it can adapt.

→
Name: Expansion of the port of Rotterdam

Location: Rotterdam, Netherlands

Date: 1400–2030

Designer: n/a

The urban landscape of Rotterdam has evolved with the changing demands for trade and shipping. The reclaiming of land from the sea allowed the port area to migrate westward to accommodate larger supertankers; the vacated docks nearer the city centre create opportunities for new land-use and urban form.

→ ↘
Name: Samarkand and Las Vegas

Location: Uzbekistan and USA

Date: n/a

Designer: n/a

These are two important cities that thrived in the context of significant routes between the East and the West. Las Vegas emerged as a stopover on the route to the Wild West and later established itself as a railroad town. In contrast, Samarkand prospered on the trade route, known as the Silk Road, between China and the Mediterranean.

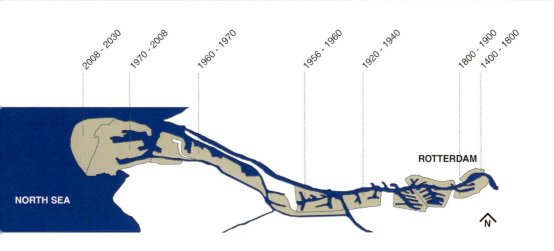

2008 - 2030   1970 - 2008   1960 - 1970   1956 - 1960   1920 - 1940   1800 - 1900   1400 - 1800

ROTTERDAM

NORTH SEA

N

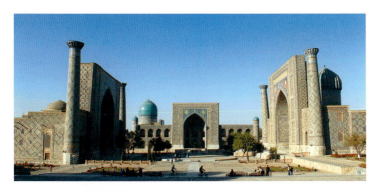

↑ →

Name: Cities of Guangdong and Shenzhen

Location: China

Date: n/a

Designer: n/a

Both cities settle in the Pearl River delta, but represent contrasting economic contexts at different moments in China's history. The province of Guangdong (above) became famous in the sixteenth century due to its exploitative colonial context. Almost 500 years later, the establishment of a Special Economic Zone (SEZ) in Shenzhen (opposite) has created a context of liberal economic laws and unprecedented urban growth.

Economic context

Economic policy can transform the context of a city. For centuries, doctrines of free trade at a global scale and tax incentives at a regional level have created changes to the city in land use and built form.

Different economic and political contexts led to the contrast in layouts between London's web of streets and the rational grid of Chicago. The top-down policy of land division and subdivision in Chicago led to a three-tiered grid pattern of 80-, 40- and 10-acre city blocks, whereas in London, the aspirations to build a more rational grid after the Great Fire of 1666 were never realised. Chicago's economic ambitions, which later led to the invention of the skyscraper, promoted the rational gridiron. On the other hand, London's complex street layout and property ownership structure led to the rebuilding of the old city based on hundreds of years of incremental economic and urban growth.

The influence of economic policy in the contemporary city is evident in the nomination of cities in categories, such as Special Economic Zones, Cities of Culture, Heritage Cities and Olympic cities. Many cities vie for these privileges, attempting to boost their growth and global profile with these new economic stimuli. For urban designers, these signify new contexts within which to design – affecting the forms, uses and spaces of the city that now must respond to the economic conditions placed upon them.

Each city provides a unique context. As a landscape architect or urban designer it is important to identify the layers that create these environments; understanding the diagram of the city as well as the image that the city projects is essential for designers working within this context.

Political contexts

Separating the political contexts from that of the economy is a formidable task. However, some city leaders are beginning to use local urban policy to distinguish their cities in national and global contexts. These individuals and their policies offer new tools and avenues for urban design. Enrique Peñalosa, Jaime Lerner and Ken Livingstone are three former mayors who have been recognised as transforming their respective cities of Bogotà, Curitiba and London. Many urban designers have worked with these city leaders in guiding policy and city-wide projects; many more have then developed proposals for specific sites within the context of new layers of policy. In the City of London, new policies have resulted in movement systems, such as London's Congestion Charge system, and, more locally, in projects such as the redesign of Trafalgar Square.

Political contexts have also contributed to the specific urban forms of Soweto in the shadow of apartheid policy; the proposals for Berlin by Hitler's architect, Albert Speer; and the modern fantasy of Lucio Costa's Brasilia. These cities are some of the most obvious examples of planning in a political context by strong and often ruthless politicians. However, as seen in Bogotà, Curitiba and London, policy-led urban design can also achieve great benefit for citizens and projects at more local scales.

'Nothing is experienced by itself, but always in relation to its surroundings, the sequence of events leading up to it, the memory of past experiences.' Kevin Lynch

The political city

The exercise of power and authority in politics often has profound implications on the spaces of the city. In particular, political decisions often result in the creation of either zones or divisions. Dramatic examples of how politics can utterly reshape an urban landscape include the Berlin Wall (separating East and West Berlin from 1961–1990) and the Green Line (separating the Turkish and Greek halves of Cyprus's capital, Nicosia).

More subtle but equally striking examples of the political shaping of cities might include Amsterdam's famous red light district, which defines an urban area unto itself for the business of sex workers, or the designations of office districts, such as London's Canary Wharf or Berlin's Potsdamer Platz. Each presumably keeps unsavoury occupations, such as prostitution or banking, at arm's length.

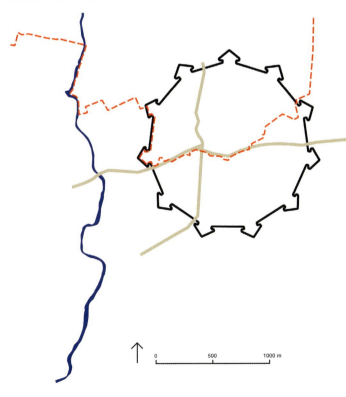

←

Name: Diagram of the divisions in Nicosia

Location: Cyprus

Date: n/a

Designer: n/a

Much of the divided city of Nicosia remains within its sixteenth-century Venetian fortifications. Within these walls, two contrasting political contexts – the Greek Cypriot community to the south and the Turkish Cypriot community to the north – have existed for several decades. A UN buffer zone – the Green Line – marks this line of separation of politics and people.

0   500   1000 m

Actions

How projects respond to the diversity of urban contexts can create new situations and scenarios in the city. For instance, the Apartheid policy in South Africa advocated the segregation of the population. This created the townships of Soweto, planned with the intention of allowing the government to control the population.

Issues of control were also fundamental to Baron Haussmann's proposals for the boulevards in Paris, which were too wide to be barricaded, but wide enough for the military to manoeuvre. The boulevards were an attempt to modernise Paris and their construction transformed the city from a collection of narrow, twisting streets into the spacious city it is today. Criticisms of this modern economic policy, the resultant new city form, and the new urban experiences are brilliantly expressed by Baudelaire in *Les Yeux des Pauvres*.

Excerpt from 'Les Yeux des Pauvres' ('The Eyes of the Poor'), from *Paris Spleen* by Charles Baudelaire

'That evening, a little tired, you wanted to sit down in front of a new café forming the corner of a new boulevard still littered with rubbish but that already displayed proudly its unfinished splendours. The café was dazzling. Even the gas burned with all the ardor of a début, and lighted with all its might the blinding whiteness of the walls, the expanse of mirrors, the gold cornices and mouldings, fat-cheeked pages dragged along by hounds on leash, laughing ladies with falcons on their wrists, nymphs and goddesses bearing on their heads piles of fruits, patés and game, Hebes and Ganymedes holding out little amphoras of syrups or parti-coloured ices; all history and all mythology pandering to gluttony.'

→

Name: Champs-Elysées

Location: Paris, France

Date: 1852–1870

Designer: Baron Georges-Eugène Haussmann

Haussmann's changes to Paris were completed in the context of the authoritarian rule of Napoléon III. Extensive changes were made to the city to demolish old quarters of the city, extend and widen boulevards, and redesign key Parisian spaces, such as Île de la Cité and Place de l'Étoile.

Systems and components

Cities are composed of interdependent systems from the city-wide scale such as transport and utilities, to the microelectronic. They support urban forms and promote opportunities for growth. These urban systems can create form in the city landscape.

Systems shape urban forms. For example, the shape of a city founded upon public transport differs radically from one built to satisfy the needs of the car. In New York, the subway follows the street network with only several feet of structure separating the road above from the tracks below. This inexpensive method of construction creates frequent apertures on the sidewalks above. These elements are missing in Moscow where the deep radial Metro network weaves separately from the gridiron of streets.

Beyond the influence of movement systems, we can anticipate the surprising effects that utility infrastructures increasingly have on a city. The availability of high-tech communications now results in clusters of businesses around certain hubs in the city; free wireless internet in public spaces blurs the separation between office, library, and public park, while in the future, localised energy production will invent new urban forms for our cities.

The systems and components of a city can create a specific context for urban design projects, offering great potential for innovations.

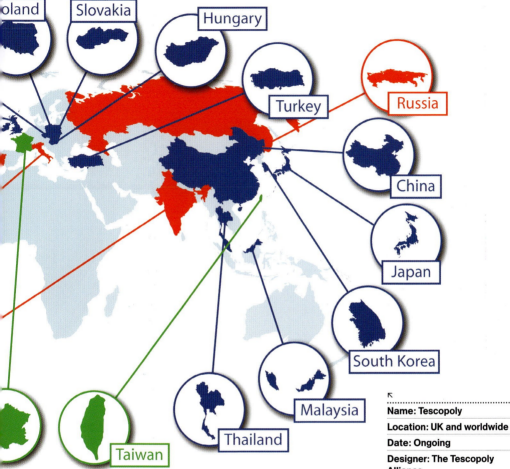

Poland · Slovakia · Hungary · Turkey · Russia · China · Japan · South Korea · Malaysia · Thailand · Taiwan

Name: Tescopoly

Location: UK and worldwide

Date: Ongoing

Designer: The Tescopoly Alliance

The supermarket chain Tesco controls over 30 per cent of the UK grocery market and its impact on cities is significant. The purple countries in the diagram represent where Tesco currently operates; red shows planned future operations; and green depicts countries from which Tesco has withdrawn. From infrastructure supply chains to building typologies, dominant industries can create and destroy urban contexts and manipulate urban policy.

The neighbourhood scale provides an immediate context for those who live in the city. Often made distinct by the particularities of the block and the street, a strong neighbourhood context accommodates and expresses the intricate complexity of daily life.

The neighbourhood context

The character of a city is derived not from individual buildings but from distinctive neighbourhoods. Neighbourhood context is fundamental to any urban design project's success. This does not mean that the project must blend in, but as with other contexts considered in urban design, the project must develop a relationship with the neighbourhood.

The factors influencing the context of a neighbourhood, and indeed the entire city, go beyond the built forms and the spaces in between. A neighbourhood is made distinct by its people, its traditions and its histories. San Telmo, the oldest barrio in Argentina, is characterised as much by its artists and tango dancers as it is by the colonial architecture and cobblestoned streets. Projects can succeed or fail based upon their ability to successfully respond to the unique context of a people and their culture.

Jane Jacobs stated that 'a successful city neighborhood is a place that sufficiently keeps abreast of its problems so it is not destroyed by them'.[1] Recognising what makes the neighbourhood in each project is the first step to understanding the context.

↑

Name: Vatnsmýri – photomontage and plan

Location: Reykjavik, Iceland

Date: Ongoing

Designer: Graeme Massie Architects

This competition-winning entry for a new neighbourhood in Reykjavik is characterised by changing arrangements of city blocks.

1. Jacobs, Jane. *The Death and Life of Great American Cities: The Failure of Town Planning.* Penguin, Harmondsworth, 1965. p. 122.

City blocks

The city block can give both neighbourhoods and cities a unique characteristic for all who live in and pass through them. The contrasting city blocks of Edinburgh's New Town and Old Town, the distinct street pattern of the West Village resisting the gridiron plan north of 14th Street in Manhattan, and the relationship between Barcelona's historic Ciutat Vella neighbourhood and the Cerda street grid are all evidence of the importance of city blocks on the urban experience.

In all three of these cities, we can find contrasting relationships between the street pattern and the city block. Historic settlements, although often clustering around roads and intersections, have allowed buildings to define the street spaces. This has resulted in many historic city centres with complex and irregular land ownership patterns, which have evolved over generations. During the Renaissance, plans for some cities in Europe began to impose rational street patterns, which in turn resulted in larger and more consistent city blocks. While Mannheim in Germany was seen as one of the first of the Renaissance cities to impose a gridiron pattern, other cities soon followed suit; new block typologies began to emerge as different grid sizes and urban relationships were explored.

The city block is often seen as a microcosm of the city. The measure of the block, the diversity of land use, the balance of open space and built form, the height, the massing and the orientation all vary to create different experiences both in the block and outside its enclosure.

In order to best understand the influence of the block, it is useful to compare the modern suburban city block with the city-centre block. The former is low in density, mono-functional and can only be accessed by car, while the latter usually contains an intricate and lively balance of uses, spaces, diversity and density. Although the suburban block can accommodate uses not seen in the city centre, the compact city block can have an intensity that creates dynamic neighbourhoods.

Urban spaces

The life of the city is frequently shown in images of new urban spaces. The relationship between people and spaces within the context of an active urban setting are what make the Zocalo in Mexico City, Central Park in New York or the South Bank in London attractive for both local people and tourists alike. These urban spaces can include the open spaces of parks, squares and courtyards, and the built form of libraries, museums and concert halls. Urban spaces can define neighbourhoods, such as Landscape Projects' design for Hulme Park in Manchester, and even cities – Times Square as emblematic of New York.

These urban elements are key to the way we perceive our cities. Michael Sorkin emphasises this in his urban manifesto, *Local Code*, where he states that each neighbourhood should have a *piazza* at its centre. On a city scale, the famous urban theorist, Kevin Lynch, describes the importance of urban spaces as 'nodes' that form a focusing part of a wider city diagram. Urban spaces define opportunities beyond the privatised realm of buildings. As urban designers, we can use urban spaces as strategic components in our plans – opportunities for creating distinct elements in the city that differentiate the extraordinary from the everyday.

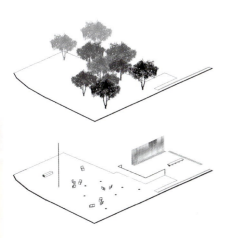

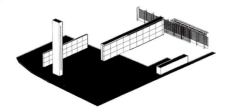

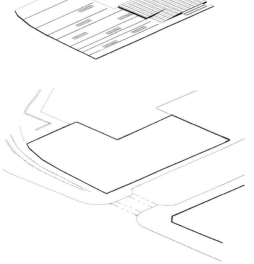

 ← ↓

Name: Whiteinch Cross – images, plan and exploded axonometric

Location: Glasgow, UK

Date: 1999

Designer: Gross Max

This small public space was designed and built for 'Glasgow 1999: UK City of Architecture and Design'. Five community spaces were constructed for this event, each attempting to engage with different parts of the city and distinct communities.

The street is the immediate life of a city. It can be the context for our understanding of many cities — the context of linkages, armatures and most importantly, the context for everyday urban experience.

Linkage

The street is an essential tool in linking urban space, bringing people and urban elements together. The connections between people and buildings that face each other across the street are important considerations for urban designers. The building mass, height, land use and street width can combine to create balanced street scenes and successful urban compositions.

The ratio of building height to street width can create contrasting images of a city. Opposition to both low-density suburban development and shade-inducing skyscrapers often advocate a 1:1 building height to street width ratio, which has been seen in the planning regulations of Washington DC and many Renaissance cities of Europe. An urban designer's awareness and manipulation of the effects of varying ratios – combined with the knowledge of the successful precedents for all types of street sections – is more important than standardised rules that may succeed in one context, but fail in others.

↑
Name: Harlem
Location: New York, USA
Date: n/a
Designer: n/a

The streets of Harlem are famous for their activity and bustle. The street hierarchies, the buildings with their stoops, the shops on the street corners and the adaptive use of the street have provided spaces for meeting outside of the cramped apartments of Harlem.

Armature

The continuous qualities of streets, blocks and infrastructure can create a framework, or armature, which connect and hold the city together. The armature at the street scale can connect urban elements. In the case of a shopping mall, two anchor stores are located at either end of an enclosed 'street'. The aim of the anchor stores is to attract customers and create a flow of shoppers between them. In turn, this footfall of potential customers attracts smaller stores to open on the armature, enhancing both the experience and the profitability of the mall. This theory, developed by Victor Gruen, is tested in malls across the United States and is evident at different scales, and with different contextual meanings in cities throughout the world.

The armature of the Royal Mile in Edinburgh, Scotland, connects Edinburgh Castle and the Palace of Holyroodhouse. While today it attracts tourist shops and bars to make it the second busiest street in the city, the historic context of the route between the castle and the abbey also attracted politicians, businessmen and philosophers alike. Other famous armatures include the Ramblas in Barcelona and Nevsky Prospekt in St Petersburg, where in the latter city, the street armature connected distant Moscow with the Neva river and the West.

↑

Name: Galleria Vittorio Emanuele II

Location: Milan, Italy

Date: 1861–1877

Designer: Giuseppe Mengoni

The Galleria Vittorio Emanuele II is a fantastic four-storey structure composed of two glass-vaulted arcades. The cruciform space of the galleria connects open spaces in the city – and the landmarks of the Duomo and the Teatro Alla Scala.

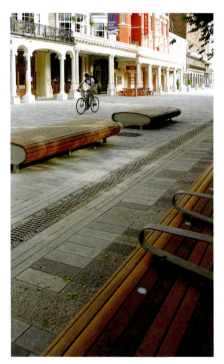

↖ ↑

Name: New Road

Location: Brighton, UK

Date: 2007

Designer: Gehl Architects / Landscape Projects

The shared space of New Road brings together pedestrians, cyclists and motor vehicles as they negotiate their way through the street.

The life of the street

The street is a social space in the city that allows for meetings and human contact. The life of the street is a concern of anthropologists, sociologists and landscape architects among many others, and it is the result of these diverse perspectives that have led to many studies of how people use street space, and the spatial context that promotes different social potential.

The narrow and labyrinthine street networks of the medieval city are seen as models for pedestrian-scale movement and social contact. Chance meetings and face-to-face contact were unavoidable in these small spaces. In contrast, the wider streets and boulevards of the eighteenth century were made to accommodate horse-drawn carriages moving at faster speeds, and were wide enough to be controlled by the military. These wide spaces, which were less conducive to social contact, began to separate flows of people with roadways and sidewalks for pedestrians. Later, cars, trains and people were fully segregated from each other, each element moving at different speeds and levels within the city. These separations were intended to enhance the efficiency of the city, but many say that this led to the 'death of the street'.

The death of the street

Urban designers in the 1950s responded to this situation by looking again at the potential of the street as the life of the city. Jane Jacobs stated that 'streets and their sidewalks, the main public spaces in the city, are its most vital organs,'[1] leading to a generation of designers aspiring to understand the importance of the life of the street and the potential that it offers.

In the 1970s, Jan Gehl responded to Jacobs and the analytical work of both Donald Appleyard and William Whyte to propose the exclusion of traffic from large areas of central Copenhagen. In opposition to several commercial interest groups that suggested this would lead to a drop in shop sales, the design interventions actually increased the footfall in the city centre and enhanced the pedestrian experience.

1. Jacobs, Jane. *The Death and Life of Great American Cities: The Failure of Town Planning.* Penguin, Harmondsworth, 1965. p. 39.

Steps, windows, trees, doorways, echoes, and reflections are only a few of the details that stimulate the senses to create a distinctive context of detail.

People and space

The details that make a city distinctive and help define its materiality – the furniture that decorates the streets or the width of the pavement – provide a rich and rewarding city experience. These details are also best seen and evaluated by the pedestrian.

While we design the environments within which we live, cities in turn direct us to use their spaces in particular ways. The reciprocal relationship between people and space has created unique contexts in cities throughout the world. New spatial typologies have emerged from traditions and cultures, while distinct urban details have evolved from environmental conditions. For example, the abundance of granite quarried in the north of Scotland led to the popularity of the material for the new buildings in Aberdeen. Visitors to the city, overwhelmed by the prevalence of this dense stone, referred to Aberdeen as the 'Granite City'.

Gordon Cullen, a key thinker on urban landscape, describes how the small elements and details seem to have a life of their own. These details that are part of the identity, history and culture of the city are also essential for promoting activities and the interaction of people in unique urban contexts throughout the world.

PROHIBITING SOCIAL CONTACT
VS.
ENHANCING SOCIAL CONTACT

SEPARATION 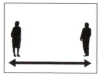 OVERLAP

DISTANCE CLOSE CONTACT

SPEED LOW SPEED

MULTIPLE LEVELS ONE LEVEL

LACK OF ORIENTATION ... SENSE OF ORIENTATION

↑
....
Name: Life Between Buildings

Location: n/a

Date: 1987

Designer: Jan Gehl

These diagrams from Jan Gehl's seminal text, *Life Between Buildings,* express the importance of spatial conditions for enhancing social contact.

↑

Name: Bus stop at New Islington

Location: Manchester, UK

Date: 2001

Designer: Grant Associates

A people-centred approach was key to the design of open spaces for the New Islington masterplan by Grant Associates. They collaborated with Alsop Architects, Ian Simpson Architects and FAT to promote concepts of colour, life and light for this 12-hectare East Manchester neighbourhood.

The markers of place

To conclude a chapter on context with a description of the markers of place is consistent with the importance of these components within a city. Many people understand their environment through the use of markers or landmarks of all different scales. At the city scale, tall buildings, bridges and monuments can make the city legible. On the other hand, small markers such as street signs or townhouse stoops provide details and key points on a journey through the city streets.

Kevin Lynch points out that landmarks are not spaces, but instead mark places in the city. While we could argue that some urban elements act as landmarks and habitable spaces, these markers of place are mostly significant for those moving through the city. These points in the landscape are references and navigators for our journey through the city – from the outer territory, the city threshold, the recognisable neighbourhood and finally, the arrival at our destination. These all rely on markers of place that create a unique map and context to every city experience.

↑

Name: Angel of the North

Location: Gateshead, UK

Date: 1998

Designer: Antony Gormley

The Angel of the North is a 20m tall and 54m wide sculpture that overlooks the A1 road and the East Coast Main Line rail route into Tyneside, UK. Much controversy surrounded the funding and construction of the sculpture. However, it has since been widely embraced as one of the most significant landmarks in northeast England.

←

Name: Street signs

Location: Andalusia, Spain

Date: n/a

Designer: n/a

Both formal and informal markers give identity to places in the landscape.

Landscape architects have a tendency to approach measure with a creative disregard. While measure in the landscape is often more subtle than that of buildings and structures, it is important to appreciate measure within the landscape architecture design process. Informed by many of the ideas in architecture and urban design, there is potential to inspire a new use of measure in landscape architecture – one that liberates the profession from arbitrary pattern making and creates a new understanding of the dimensions that make up the landscape.

A measure is simply a unit or standard of measurement. We are used to understanding our designs internationally in relation to metric units. However, we must also understand less tangible measures, such as the measures of nature, the measures of social space, and the measures of time and rhythm that overlap to define the city. This chapter explores both the measures of the landscape that inform the design of cities and the urban measures that, in turn, inform the design of wider landscape spaces.

←
....
Name: Avalanche Barriers

Location: Siglufjordur, Iceland

Date: 1999

Designer: Hnit and Landslag

From the measure of the building to the measure of a mountain – to the destructive speed and mass of an avalanche – getting the right measure is crucial in urban design.

The simple measures of the street are in its width, height and length. These measures can collectively and individually give distinction to our experience of moving through the streets. Understanding what requirements dictate these measures allows the urban designer to engage with the spatial dimensions of the city.

Enclosure

The enclosure of urban spaces can often define the feel of a city. The sense of enclosure and unfolding sequence created by the streets of Rome contribute to the experience of this ancient city. They are in contrast to the oversized boulevards being built in Dubai. Although, of course, other factors contribute to our experience of a place, as urban designers we should understand what measures and dimensions create these unique experiences. The three measures that create the enclosure of the street include: the width of the street, the height of the building, and the length of the view along the street. The relationships or ratios between these measurements are important. The ratios 1:1, 2:1, 4:1, or even greater building-height to street-width ratios, can alternate the sense of enclosure and dictate the overall experience of the city.

There are also social considerations that are greatly affected by the dimensions of street spaces. In his book *Life Between Buildings*, Jan Gehl describes what he called 'the social field of vision along the length of a street'.[1] In the study, he records how the distance between individuals affects their interactions with each other. At distances of up to 1km, one can recognise the form of another person. At 30m apart, one can begin to see and understand the other person's 'primary feelings'; and not until one is as close as 3m away can we begin to communicate normally with this person. These measures can have a significant influence on the design of our social street spaces.

1. Gehl, Jan. *Life Between Buildings*. Arkitektens Forlag. 2001. p. 67.

↑

Name: Memorial to the murdered Jews of Europe

Location: Berlin, Germany

Date: 2003–2005

Designer: Peter Eisenman

The space within this memorial is intended to create a sense of self-conscious discomfort or unease appropriate to the remembrance of a global tragedy. The qualities of a space's enclosure can also be used to create the opposite effect – to make an urban space welcoming and embracing.

↑

Name: Street enclosure

Location: Milan, Italy

Date: n/a

Designer: n/a

The historic city-centre streets of many European cities provide shade from the summer sun and a pedestrian-scale enclosure.

Circulation

A city is experienced in motion. It therefore makes sense that our streets are, in part, a measure of these movement systems. The *New Metric Handbook* details how 5.5m is the width required for any two vehicles in the UK to pass each other; parking spaces on the street are 1.8m wide, and the sidewalk width can vary depending on how many people are required to walk side by side. These dry specifications begin to reveal that subtle changes in measure can have a significant urban influence. Narrowing road width and tightening street corner radius can reduce the speed of car traffic on a street. Measure is important to mass transit as well. For example, trams require platforms that accommodate both the tram length and the height of the tram floor. This impacts on those who drive or ride trams in the city, and allows pedestrians to traverse the street unimpeded by high platforms, wide crossings and fast roadways.

New circulation systems should anticipate future forms of movement in the city. The measure of these systems could be the key to their success. Should bicycles or high-speed trains be the new street measure? Should cars adapt to fit the city? Should the city slow down to the measure of a child's walking pace? A big vision and many small adjustments will be required of urban designers for cities to accommodate circulation needs in the future.

↑ →
....

Name: Flower Power Project

Location: Schiphol / Haarlemmermeer / Haarlem, Netherlands

Date: 1988–2002

Designer: Nio Architecten

This transport project by Nio Architecten responds to the measure of bus transport, although its artistic forms are not restricted by it. Tunnels, viaducts and other built structures make navigating the area both an adventure and a delight.

→

Name: Historic map of Edinburgh

Location: Edinburgh, UK

Date: n/a

Designer: n/a

The Royal Mile, measured as approximately 1.8km in length, was the equivalent of the old Scottish mile. It runs between the Palace of Holyroodhouse and the castle.

Armature

The measures within the structural armature of a city can be read at different scales. The linear armature of the street is an important device for promoting movement between urban hubs. Therefore, the length of the street is important for establishing these movements and relationships. The archetype of the mall, invented by Victor Gruen, proposed the split-level street armature with an optimum length of 600 ft (183m). It was believed that this measure was the best for sustaining the interest of the shopper. This concept of an optimum length for shopping street armature has maintained currency even as the importance of the traditional outdoor high street has re-emerged in recent decades.

In *Recombinant Urbanism*, David Grahame Shane follows Gruen's measure of 600 ft (183m), but elaborates to describe the measure of compressed armatures to be 450 ft (137m) and stretched armatures, such as the Las Vegas Strip that promotes the use of motor vehicles, to have a measure of 2.5 miles (4km) between the airport and downtown. The extent of Shane's discussion of armatures reaches beyond that of the street to also show vertical armatures in the skyscrapers of the city. His interpretations of the armature as an urban device with multiple applications demonstrate a simple, but extremely flexible model.

→ ↘
···

Name: Armature diagrams

Location: n/a

Date: n/a

Designer: David Grahame Shane

These diagrams of linear armatures, as featured in the book *Recombinant Urbanism*, represent the potential of the linear armature as a measure in the city.

STANDARD ARMATURE DIAGRAM

COMPRESSED ARMATURE DIAGRAM

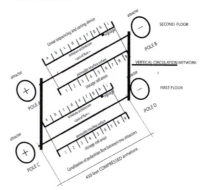

STRETCHED ARMATURE DIAGRAMS

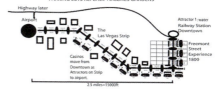

The armature measure can be seen in both planned and unplanned cities. The Royal Mile in Edinburgh connects the Palace of Holyroodhouse and the castle, while in Liverpool the historic armature of Hope Street connects the two great cathedrals that are positioned at either end. To understand a street that functions as an armature, we must understand the distances between the urban attractors and the methods for moving between them. Creating a network of points and lines across the city can expose the possibilities for moving through it, affecting the legibility of the experience, and the success of the city's design.

While the pattern of the city block may make the city plan distinctive, the measure of the block has greater repercussions on the life of the city.

City functions: land use and city life

The measure of the city block is one of the most significant measures in the city. Through dividing and subdividing the urban plan, the mass of the city block is offset by the void of the street space. The measure of the block can influence the typology, height, density, massing, and rhythm of a building. The block impacts on city life in the land-use patterns of the buildings and the street.

The typical city block is enclosed by a boundary of public streets. This boundary restricts the expansion of buildings and activities. It is unusual for functions to extend beyond the block boundary. Land-use activities follow models for their location, size and operation. When the city block constrains the expansion of a particular land use, the building typology is forced to innovate to fit the block measure.

As a result of the relationship between the measure of the block and the land-use patterns of the city, it is unusual to find 'big-box' retail areas, conference centres, casino hotels, sports stadiums and airports within historic urban centres. Where these elements have been able to adapt to the city, one might find local supermarkets, boutique hotels or small casinos. However, when large companies and their requirements for big footprint development cannot adapt or spread beyond the boundaries of the city block, new development patterns emerge outside the city. The superblock measure of modernist plans, such as that for Milton Keynes in England and its 1km square blocks, allows for the low-density spread of these new urban forms. Since the development of these suburban models during the 1900s, there has been a draw of populations from the city centres to automobile-dominated environments on the outskirts of the city.

↓ →
....

Name: Brixton town centre interchange – model and plans

Location: London, UK

Date: 2000

Designer: Space Syntax

The measure of building typologies and city blocks can determine the possible land-uses for urban developments. This project assessed existing and potential routes through Brixton to release new sites for development.

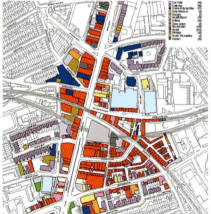

Mass, massing and bulk

The Battery Park design guidelines for the North Residential Neighborhood describe bulk as 'the density of development and the configuration of buildings on the parcels'.[1] Also described as massing, the bulk of a city block can have a variety of effects on the city at many different scales. The experience of the street can be defined by the sense of enclosure created by the length of the street wall, or by the amount of light permeating between the tall buildings of a block. The experience of the city, on the other hand, can be created by the skyline composed of certain building mass, or by the density of buildings compressed onto the city block.

The measure of these elements is an important consideration in contemporary planning and zoning. Bulk controls that consider height, block coverage and building setback are criticised at times for being too prescriptive, while the zoning of blocks using floor area ratio (FAR) calculations are deemed too open for interpretation by architects, and do not protect the scale or character of neighbourhoods. The FAR is simply the total building area divided by the site area. The use of FAR ratios allows the architect to choose between low-rise buildings that cover a greater area of the site or taller buildings that have a smaller footprint.

The creative interpretations of built form on the urban block must be explored to enliven the city. FARMAX, a speculation into the relationship between FAR and population density by the urbanists at MVRDV, provides a refreshing perspective on the relationships and consequences of measure in built form. Whether described as the bulk, mass or form of the city block, we must remember that the measure of heights, lengths and setbacks of buildings that make up these definitions also create many of the spaces, and define our experience of the built urban public realm.

↑ ↘
....

Name: Alcoi – image, model and plan

Location: Alicante, Spain

Date: 2001

Designer: Manuel de Solà-Morales

Nestled within the old quarter of the city, this residential project mimics and responds to the historic measures of the urban form.

1. Lerner, Ralph. *Design Guidelines for the North Residential Neighborhood.* Battery Park City Authority. 1994. p. 44.

Rhythm

When moving through the city, the rhythm of spaces and buildings gives delight to the senses. Both repeating and varying measures of the city block can provide texture to the many ways we experience the street. A square grid creates the same rhythm in both directions of the grid. Variations in rhythm are found in cities with more than one street plan measure, such as the 1857 plan of Chicago that combines blocks of 80, 50 and 10 acres. Another example is the plan of Detroit that overlays the famous Mile Roads over a grid of smaller city blocks. However, it is not only the gridiron city plan that creates distinct urban rhythms. Edwin Lutyens's New Delhi uses varying block measures to generate a unique experience while driving through the city.

The positions of landmarks or individual buildings can also create rhythm. Rhythm can also be found in the activity of the city – from the sun's course across the sky to the tide of commuters moving along the sidewalk. Whether standing still as these rhythms pass around you or riding through the designed city – rhythm is a unique component of all urban life.

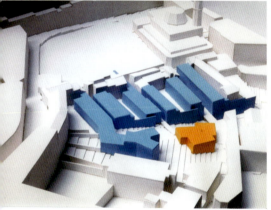

Many measures can inform the design of buildings and open spaces. Measures that are required by planning and building authorities can be as significant as those that provide a conceptual framework for the design process.

Typologies

'Form follows function' is a statement associated with the great American architect, Louis Sullivan. While there have been decades of debate as to whether this modernist proposition is true, in urban design proposals building forms need to fit the scale of intended typologies and land use. Understanding the characteristics of different typologies, specifically their measures, allows proposed forms to be drawn accurately.

Technical manuals, such as *The New Metric Handbook* or *Timesaver Standards for Landscape Architecture*, illustrate standardised units and functions of different building and open-space typologies. This allows us to gauge measures such as how the optimum length of a hotel corridor could maximise efficiency and profit, or how the minimum size of an urban park can act effectively to promote a bio-diverse habitat. Comparing different typologies can help the designer anticipate the future functions of the city and how the city might change over time.

The width of a row of townhouses provides more entrances onto the street than an apartment building that fills a block, and that may have only one entrance. The former townhouse block may promote more interpersonal contact along the stoops, while the apartment typology allows for higher density that may also animate the street. Adapting a townhouse typology for other non-residential uses might be restricted to small restaurants, stores and offices that could use these small spaces. However, in the larger apartment typology that occupies the measure of the city block, these spaces could be divided and subdivided for other potential uses, such as office or workshop space.

Either or both of these typologies might be appropriate to a given setting, and it is the task of the urban designer to balance form and function within the urban fabric.

↑ ↙ ↓

Name: Breevaarthoek

Location: Gouda, Netherlands

Date: 2001

Designer: KCAP

The edge condition of this landscape has been used as a point of departure. This mixed-use proposal incorporates several different residential typologies and commercial space.

Density

The density of the city is defined by the number of people occupying a given area of land. Density may also compare the number of individual dwellings or habitable rooms in a specific area.

Common studies of density compare the built-up urban centres to the diffuse outlying suburbs, where typically there are fewer buildings per hectare than in the city centre. These, however, express the density of buildings and not the population or residential density. While density may be seen in the building forms that create a distinct skyline, the experience of the city is in the way it functions and how it is inhabited.

Higher-density cities may well be more sustainable, though this can be seen as counter-intuitive. Low-density suburbs tend to be car dependent, whereas high densities allow goods and services to be concentrated and close-at-hand while supporting the use of public mass transportation.[1] Javier Mozas and Aurora Fernandez Per, the authors of the book *Density*, support the latter position. In their book, they compare different measures of density and how these affect transportation.

They state that Los Angeles has an average density of 15 dwellings per hectare although 'the minimum recommendable density for providing a bus service is 25', and a density of 60 dwellings per hectare 'is required to warrant the installation of a tram service'. These statistics suggest that there are thresholds of density that can promote different ways for the city to function – these thresholds can be important tools in urban design.

1. Mozas, Javier and Fernandez Per, A. *Density: New Collective Housing*. a + t ediciones, Vitoria-Gasteiz and Madrid, 2006.

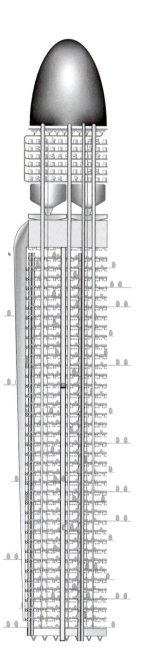

← ↖
....
Name: Pig City

Location: Rotterdam, Netherlands

Date: 2001

Designer: MVRDV

This project explores the premise of transforming pig farming in vertical structures to improve animal welfare, productivity and land efficiency.

↑
....
Name: The Porter House, 336 West 15th Street

Location: New York, USA

Date: 2003

Designer: SHoP Architects

A renovated warehouse with a cantilevered four-storey addition (top left of image) provides a dramatic landmark in the city.

Height

A floor-to-floor vertical measure of 3–4m is a good guide for buildings in urban design plans. Unfortunately, as a rule of thumb, it oversimplifies the importance of building heights in the design of the city. Building heights affect the amount of sun that may penetrate through to the street, provide enclosure for urban spaces, influence the balance of height-to-width street ratios, and impact on the development of land-use patterns. The heights of buildings also form the skyline – and with it a certain image of the city.

The ten-storey Home Insurance Building, built in Chicago in 1885, is cited as the world's first skyscraper. The new steel-framed construction type, along with the invention of the safety elevator, allowed habitable buildings to push ever upwards. While ten-storey apartment buildings existed even in ancient Rome, the upper floors were typically rented to the lower classes due to the inconvenience of climbing to the higher floors. Tall buildings have always been expressions of power, control and prosperity. The pyramids of Egypt, the towers of Bologna, the great European cathedrals, or the town halls of industrial England were assertions of dominion that are no different from the Petronas Towers in Kuala Lumpur and the Gherkin in London.

↑

Name: Jianwai SOHO

Location: Beijing, China

Date: 2004

Designer: Riken Yamamoto and Field Shop

This mixed-use complex of high-density buildings reaches up to 31 storeys in height, filling the skyline with giant forms.

While the measure of these individual buildings generates an image of the city and contributes to famous skylines around the world, the measure of buildings of a consistent height can also have implications for the city. Skyscrapers squander much energy in order to pump water to higher floors, to light lower floors that receive insufficient natural light, and to propel people in lifts between the many levels. Therefore, building typologies such as the six-storey, 'walk-up' apartment building, as found in many New York City neighbourhoods, could promote a more consistent and equally dense urban plan. In Lower Manhattan during the early 1900s, the increase in the number of tall buildings began to turn streets into dark chasms. The Equitable Life Building occupied almost a whole city block and caused outrage in New York, ultimately leading to the introduction of the 'setback zoning policy'. The setback is evident in the subsequent design of the Empire State Building, where the upper floors of the building are stepped back from the street edge, allowing more light and ventilation into the adjacent plots and city spaces. With the passing of the setback zoning laws, the measure of building height began to dictate the measure of the other two building dimensions: width and depth.

Inhabitation of the city requires an understanding of human measures. These measures can inform details and experiences that make a city particularly distinctive.

The measure of the person

Until the international recognition of the decimalised system of measurement in the 1960s, our standard of measurements often contained explicit reference to the measure of the human body.

Although urban design does not usually consider the subtle measures associated with the physical dimensions of a person, there are instances when a small urban measure can have wider implications. The height of a kerb is a noteworthy example. A typical kerb dimension may be 150mm in height, and vary between raised kerbs of up to 250mm and flush kerbs that are level with the road and the sidewalk. The raised kerb is a useful edge that deters the movement of cars from the roadway to the sidewalk, but it is not so high that it restricts pedestrian movement. However, the raised kerb could also suggest that the pedestrian is subservient to the motor vehicle. Recent projects by Landscape Projects and Gehl Architects in Brighton, UK, and by Camlin Lonsdale in Manchester, UK, have addressed this issue by proposing flush kerbs between the sidewalk and the roadway, and creating shared surface movement spaces on some streets.

The height and tread dimensions of steps can also promote movement between parts of the city and can provide informal theatres. The dimensions and proportions of the 138 steps of the famous Spanish Steps in Rome are supposed to provide one of the most comfortable experiences of climbing steps. These distances – social spaces where people can meet, the measure between two seats, or the height of a tree canopy on a boulevard – are intricate human measures in urban design, and can affect movement and function within the city.

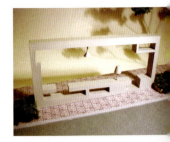

↑

Name: The Roppongi Hills Streetscape Project

Location: Roppongi Hills, Japan

Date: 2003

Designer: Various

Experimental forms provide seating and social spaces. These seats respond to the measure of a person while suggesting new social arrangements.

→

Name: Central-Mid-Levels Escalator

Location: Hong Kong, China

Date: 1993

Designer: n/a

The world's longest covered escalator links central Hong Kong with the residential area of the Mid-Levels. Its great scale obscures the fact that it is designed for the scale of the individual commuter.

↑

Name: Spanish Steps

Location: Rome, Italy

Date: c1717

Designer: Francesco de Sanctis

The Spanish Steps (Scalinata della Trinità dei Monti) famously ascend the steep slope between the Piazza di Spagna and the Trinità dei Monti. The flight of 138 steps responds to both the measure of the city and the measure of the human step.

Walking

The measure of a person is not read only in the physical dimensions of the human body. The motion of the city dweller engaging with the spaces and systems of the city can also be measured to inform urban design decisions.

Measures of movement, such as the distance that a person will choose to walk, impact how urban designers plan the future city. They are also important indicators of the size of communities and neighbourhoods. Some designers propose a maximum distance of 1km between key places in the city – school, work and the local shops. This threshold is distorted when key places are not designed to accommodate pedestrians. Supermarkets, shopping malls, multiplex cinemas and the land-use typologies synonymous with the suburbs often do not accommodate pedestrian access at all. These destinations require a car and promote a migration from local community facilities to those that sit on the edge of the city.

In their contribution to the book, *Sustainable Urban Design*, Robert Thorne and William Filmer-Sankey examine the concept of the walkable community.[1] The measures they illustrate for a neighbourhood are up to 600m, and up to 2km for a city district. This commitment to specific units is useful for comparing the potentials of different urban measures, and essential to examining the successes and failures of walking as an effective urban measure.

1. Thorne, R & Filmer-Sankey, W. 'Transportation' in Thomas, R (Ed). *Sustainable Urban Design*. Spons, 2003.

Commuting

The journey between home and work is a daily pilgrimage that bookends a working day. There are many dimensions to a commute including time, distance, station transfers, cost, travel modes and travel companions. Each defines how long, far, simple, expensive, luxurious and cramped our journey to work is.

If we compare the commuting infrastructure of New York City with London, there are several measures that are argued to affect each city. First, the New York subway has a flat-fare system – the ticket price is the same for travelling two stops and travelling to the end of the line. This flat-fare increases the mobility of both city residents and workers, facilitating greater movement between neighbourhoods, and reducing the segregation of communities.

On the other hand, London has a series of zones that radiate from the centre, and each zone has an ascending ticket price as one moves out from the centre.

The 24-hour operation of the subway in New York allows the city to operate more fluidly, whereas London's Tube network closes every night for about five hours. New York City's airports, railroad stations, hospitals, convenience stores and population of service workers do not need to anticipate the closing times of its public transport system.

The distance and time of a commute can be transformed when the design of districts, blocks and buildings allows for workers to live close by. The frequency, speed, and capacity of future movement systems will let us plan the city with guides that transcend the design of urban space. The measure of the commute can create new rhythms and urban experiences, which enhance the beginning and end of each day – wherever and whenever those experiences may be.

↑
Name: New York City subway map

Location: New York, USA

Date: 1979

Designer: Michael Hertz Associates

Although the New York City subway map designed by Massimo Vignelli is considered a design classic, the most recent incarnation of the map is deemed to be more geographically accurate. This shows the subway lines that predominantly follow the street grid patterns, reaching from the Bronx to Brooklyn on a single fare.

Local networks

Local networks have become useful tools in the promotion of urban systems that aspire to social, economic and environmental sustainability. Therefore, tools that increase social contact, maintain the flow of capital and resources, and sustain a lively community, can be accurately promoted and understood.

In many ways, local networks are the systems in which people have lived for millennia, but we have become more separated from these systems as power generation and food production have become ever more remote.

There is little value in planning communities in isolation. The local network is unworkable in isolation from wider networks that support, influence and supply local flows. The encounter of the future city is in its unique positioning between closeness and distance, weaving the two in exciting and unexpected combinations.

Two recent projects, BedZED in south London, UK and Bo01 in Malmö, Sweden, have transformed their local networks into a tool for facilitating different sustainable ambitions. For BedZED, a 55km radius was set for the sourcing of bulky construction materials, while electric vehicles that supply food boxes from local farms to the residents have a range of 40km. In Bo01, similar plans to manage 100 per cent of waste on site and generate 100 per cent of energy within close proximity to the development were overlaid with designs for a mixed-use development creating a sustained local economy and social network.

These local networks may remind us of the pedestrian-scaled city blocks promoted by Jane Jacobs. However, they have evolved as complex hybrids of local and distant influences. The measure of the local is critical to understand, and how this engages with wider networks will allow us to anticipate our potential experiences in the contemporary city.

The measure of infrastructure and utilities is not always immediately evident in the form of the city. However, when looking closely, these measures have a real and distinct influence on the spaces created and the experiences of city inhabitants.

Infrastructure

Infrastructures are fundamental facilities, systems, or frameworks that organise or service society and its settlements. Public utilities are part of city, country and regional infrastructure that provide essential services such as water, electricity and gas.

There are three measures to be considered. First is the diversity of infrastructures in the city that give options for the city user; second is the quantity or capacity of these infrastructures (including the number of users); and finally, there is coverage that indicates the area serviced.

Diversity

The diversity of infrastructures provides options for people living in and experiencing the city. Mechanised transport is a visible infrastructure found in cities throughout the world. Some citizens have numerous options for moving around the city, while others are limited to one or two modes. Cars, buses, trams, underground trains, overland trains and elevated trains are some of the options in a typical city, while water and air transport can add additional layers of complexity to a system. We have seen that different urban densities will allow for different modes of transport – so we can begin to understand the relationships between urban densities and transport options.

Communications infrastructure has become increasingly present in our cities. The choices from pay phone to mobile phone, or dial-up internet to wireless broadband, are only a few examples of how methods of communication have rapidly changed. The availability of new digital communications and the multiple options for this exchange are changing the way in which people work and live in the city. Remote servers allow for working at home as easily as wireless internet in public spaces transports the office into the park, while forms that relate to infrastructures (public pay phones, for example) are becoming obsolete. It is important, though, to maintain elements of redundancy in systems, both to prevent monopolies and to ensure that services remain available even if one system is compromised.

↑

Name: Transport options

Location: Detroit, USA

Date: n/a

Designer: n/a

A diversity of transport infrastructure options is essential for the city. When the trams were removed and the main station in Detroit (Michigan Central Station) closed, there were few options for the residents of the Motor City.

Capacity

Issues arising from the measure of infrastructure confront us daily. When the broadband download speed drops at certain times of the day, or when traffic becomes congested even though there is no accident in sight, we can presume that part of the system is reaching capacity. These issues have been summarised as 'supply and demand' – where the levels of demand for a service approach those of the supply to the infrastructure.

Increasing the capacity of infrastructures is important for the growth of cities and great efforts have been made to achieve this. Many redevelopment projects are motivated by the apparent need to expand before full capacity is reached. Examples include new highway projects such as Robert Moses' proposal to increase road capacity in New York, and the controversial plans to build a third runway at London's Heathrow Airport.

It is a maxim that building new roads to relieve traffic congestion is like 'fighting obesity by letting out one's belt'. Wider roads simply seem to increase the demand for road space. There are also debates about whether it is sustainable for cities to continually provide greater infrastructure capacity to promote further urban growth. The increased competition between distant cities is key to this. However, more emphasis could be placed on the innovation of infrastructure than on increasing capacity. Many water-scarce cities are realising this with new methods for water management gaining importance over transporting water from afar, while traffic-congested cities are looking to road pricing measures that can return finance to mass-transit innovation.

↑ ↗ →

Name: Ford's River Rouge Factory

Location: Detroit, USA

Date: 2004

Designer: William McDonough + Partners and Arcadis Giffels

The future of infrastructure will likely require a more local focus. Transporting essential services, such as water and electricity, over great distances is simply not a long-term option. The Ford River Rouge factory makes great strides with, among other measures, its enormous living roof, which deals with stormwater management, provides habitat, generates oxygen, and insulates the building.

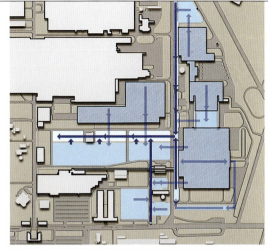

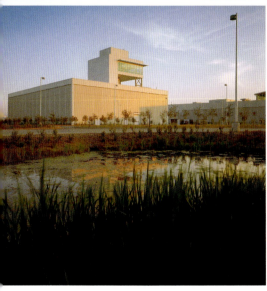

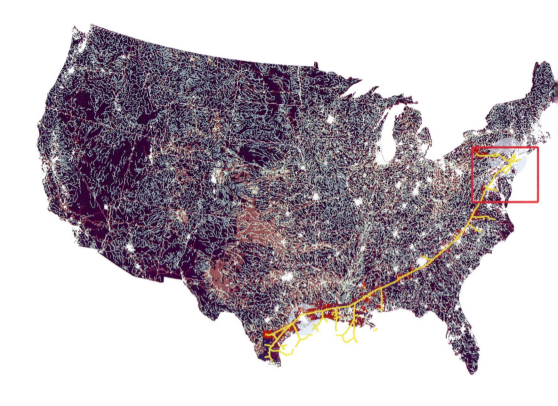

↑ ↗
....

**Name: Deterritorialising
Infrastructure, Repositioning
Urbanism**

Location: USA

Date: 2005

Designer: Petia Morozov

The Transco pipeline and
various macro systems of
organisation inform each other's
routes of distribution in mutually
modifying patterns. These
drawings, by Petia Morozov, are
part of a research project.

Coverage

Coverage is best explained by looking at mobile phone networks. Typically, there is a dense map of coverage around heavily populated urban centres, and patchy coverage in the remote and less-inhabited corners of the country. This is a perennial phenomenon in electricity, gas, water, transport and communications infrastructures, as the cost of providing infrastructure far exceeds returns to the infrastructure or utility companies. These issues have been exaggerated further with recent neo-liberal economic policy that promotes the privatisation of once-public services. Infrastructure that was once perceived as a collective good, such as transport, water and electricity, has been increasingly privatised. This is usually to the detriment of the public good, as this places more value on shareholder profit than on service provision.

The resultant fracturing of infrastructural coverage is the topic of a recent book called *Splintering Urbanism* by Stephen Graham and Simon Marvin. This changing landscape has led to new communications, such as broadband, only being available in large cities. Meanwhile, older infrastructures, such as national train networks, are becoming difficult to maintain due to reduced public subsidy and increased emphasis on profit. These processes promote social and financial segregation, while further dislocating the city from its territory.

Will parts of the future city require water vendors, similar to those in Nigeria's capital, Abuja? The BBC has reported that the cost of water from these essential and informal vendors is many times more in Manila, Philippines and Accra, Ghana than what is paid by Londoners and New Yorkers to their respective utility companies. Wealthy neighbourhoods have begun to live 'off the grid' in gated communities and exclusive developments. Can urban designers promote alternatives to this break-up?

'It is perhaps paradoxical that the initial rambling and sifting through an immense, open-ended landscape would lead us to something as precise and determinate as measure.'
James Corner

Cities are shaped as much by movement as they are by buildings, and as movement and transportation occur in the landscape, they are the natural concern of landscape architects. Movement includes the transport of goods, the distribution of services and the daily movements of individuals around their neighbourhoods, and between home and work. The character of an urban space is often determined by the types, manners and speeds of flow through it.

All methods of travelling through the city are known as modes and these include walking, cycling, driving and public transport. Walkability is key to good urban design; individuals require quality, ease of movement and access to facilities in and around their neighbourhoods.

←
....
Name: Kai Tak Airport

Location: Hong Kong, China

Date: 1993

Designer: n/a

Movement can shape and occupy cities in very dramatic ways.

Movement has had a profound effect on urban form over the ages. This effect has often been explosive in speed rather than incremental, as great changes in urban spaces have been caused by new innovations in transportation. The invention of the railroad and the automobile, in particular, made sweeping changes in the structure and form of our cities.

Early

Early settlements, such as Çatalhöyük in Anatolia, showed few, if any, streets and the majority of movement would have probably been across rooftops and in courtyards. The street as we know it – a place for transportation of goods, commerce, meeting and exchange – was at one point an innovation. Streets, together with buildings, have formed the framework for urban structure for millennia and changes to this structure have been incremental. These changes often responded to innovation in transportation modes, from travel on foot to horseback travel, chariots to oxcarts and the carriage to the car, plane and bullet train.

Movement by sea and by inland waterways have also had a profound impact on the development of urban form. Canals can be classified as forms of streets. Rivers, even the widest and most majestic, can serve as streets, with bridges and tunnels connecting the sidewalks and buildings on either side. Ports and waterways have been strong determinants for both the siting of cities and their ultimate form, and just as road-going vehicles have changed over time, so have watercraft, often necessitating massive changes in urban landscapes.

↑

Name: Lingotto Fiat Factory

Location: Turin, Italy

Date: 1916–1923

Designer: Mattè Trucco

At the Lingotto factory, cars were assembled over five ramped floors and completed at the top where a test track was located.

LIVERPOOL

MANCHESTER

RIVER MERSEY

MANCHESTER SHIP CANAL

N

Industrial

The Industrial Revolution utterly changed the distribution of population across the landscape. In England, particularly in Lancashire, rural areas were seemingly emptied overnight, and populations migrated to the cities to work in the 'dark, satanic mills'. This was the age of steam, steel and the great textile mills of the Midlands and Industrial North. The incredible flow of humanity into the cities expanded their size exponentially; at the same time, it also exacerbated the problems of very high-density slums.

The exploitation of fossil fuels for transportation allowed for rapid advances in the speed, distance, and efficiency of travel and transport. The brute force of steam trains and steam ships were matched by Herculean achievements in the building and engineering of transportation infrastructure. Where previously roads, natural waterways and narrow streets funnelled people and goods into the city, now great canals and viaducts transected the landscape, and ports grew ever larger. In cities, the terminals for these transportation links reorganised the traditional spaces, shifting emphasis from the old market squares, cathedrals and political centres to spaces that celebrated movement and speed. Railways, or the lack of them, could spell life or death for towns, and often they created entirely new settlements wherever they pushed into virgin territory. However, this centralisation of transportation was to be threatened at the end of the nineteenth and early twentieth centuries by the increasing popularity of two inventions that fundamentally changed the way people moved through the city: the bicycle and the motorcar.

↑

Name: Manchester Ship Canal diagram

Location: Lancashire, UK

Date: 1887–1896

Designer: Hamilton Fulton, Edward Leader Williams

The Manchester Ship Canal was an important shipping link between Manchester, the Port of Liverpool and the markets of the world. Large transportation infrastructure such as this has the power to shape not just local, but also regional and global urban form.

Modern

The stories of the modern city and the motorcar are inseparable. Perhaps no other invention has had such a profound, sometimes fortuitous, but more often calamitous impact upon the shape and function of cities in all of history. Discourse about urban form and function throughout the twentieth century and to the present day has been dominated by the impact of the private automobile. In addition, a tension developed between those engineers and planners who worked with infrastructure for the car and those planners and designers concerned with urban environmental quality, which often was a question of human health and well-being.

Traffic is not a new phenomenon. The invention of the street made congestion possible and history is full of traffic jams, whether flocks of sheep and geese, or the horse-drawn carriages of the wealthy. The car created traffic, however, that was more dangerous than ever before. The speed and size of cars made their impact lethal, and this, more than any issues with pollution, made it desirable to enforce a separation between cars and pedestrians. The conventional street grid that had served cities so well for millennia, now became undesirable. Car traffic began to be served by small 'feeder' roads that served large arterial roads created with one goal in mind: speed. Cities such as Milton Keynes in England or Chandigarh in India took on an utterly new and idealised form based upon providing totally separate spaces for cars and people.

With more people piloting individual vehicles into the city, it became necessary to find places to store them when they were not in use. Parking, over time, became seen as more of a right than a privilege. To this day, the provision of car parking, or the lack thereof, can often fuel the most heated of civic debates. Parking was to become as much a dominant urban form as architecture, especially where land was cheap.

For all their faults, cars symbolised freedom, status and sex appeal. The dream of the open road brought people in contact with wider landscapes than ever before, possibly increasing an understanding and appreciation of the landscape.

↑

Name: General Motors Futurama Exhibit, 1939–40 New York World's Fair

Location: New York, USA

Date: 1939

Designer: Norman Bel Geddes

The Futurama exhibit combined sprawling suburbs with a massive, automated interstate highway system. It was a taste of things to come, but a utopian vision of what would become dystopic. General Motors did eventually design a working automated highway, but this has not yet become a reality.

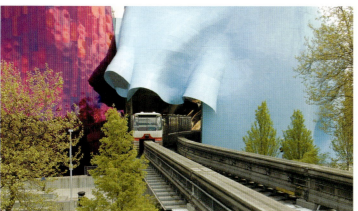

←

Name: Experience Music Project (EMP)

Location: Seattle, USA

Date: 2000

Designer: Frank Gehry

While far from Gehry's most distinguished work, the EMP mixes optimistic and imaginative contemporary architecture with the equally optimistic monorail – a legacy of the 1962 Seattle World's Fair. The same fair gave us the most elegant observation tower of any city: the Space Needle.

← ↓ →

Name: Terminus Hoenheim-Nord

Location: Strasbourg, France

Date: 2001

Designer: Zaha Hadid

Hadid's austere design brings together the trajectories of pedestrians, bicycles, cars and trams in overlapping fields and lines. It is a park-and-ride scheme that seeks to reduce traffic congestion in Strasbourg.

Contemporary

The symbolism of the car has changed radically in the last couple of decades. The dream of the open road has given way to the reality of bondage in gridlock and the grinding daily commute. We now know that the often invisible pollution from cars could be making us as sick as did the choking green fogs of the Industrial Revolution. After the Second World War in the United States, the powerful major industries associated with oil, cars and road building began the process of either actively buying up and dismantling public transportation and freight infrastructure (such as streetcar lines and rail freight), or lobbying for their replacement with roads, cars and lorries. These patterns were replicated internationally, as the decentralisation of transport created great opportunities for the concentration of wealth. However, these industries are increasingly under fire for the long-term damage that they do. Designers, planners, scientists and engineers are now seeking new ways of building transportation that allow people at least a modicum of the choice offered by cars, while creating solutions that are ecologically, environmentally and socially sustainable.

Public transportation has emerged once again to be recognised as an option for urban transportation that can be comfortable, pleasant and efficient. New methods of consolidating and organising urban freight deliveries are being tested in many cities and often, old, existing, or abandoned infrastructure, such as canals, are being reinhabited for the purpose. The dogma of separating cars from pedestrians is also being challenged, often with great success, as shared space schemes are tried in many cities.

The speed at which one travels affects the experience and understanding of the landscape during the journey. Even at the neighbourhood level, if one person walks regularly while another drives, their understanding of their locale will be strikingly different.

Slow

The city is always in motion, and the common perception is that the pace at which it operates is frenetic and unrelenting. A well-designed city, however, leaves plenty of options for moving slowly and graciously. The nineteenth-century French poet, Charles Baudelaire, wrote about a particular type of walker in Paris: the *flâneur*. The *flâneur* used strolling through the city as a way of savouring the urban experience. They moved slowly, drifting through the streets and arcades of Paris, breathing in all the activities, and watching the parade of fascinating people that the city invariably provided. While the *flâneur* was a product of the time, the idea should not strike us as odd, given that we are now encouraged to travel to cities as tourists and absorb them in much the same way. Contemplation is a natural adjunct to stimulation in the city, and probably a necessary antidote to it.

Good urban design should allow many different scales and speeds of movement to occur and coexist. Parks and shopping areas are excellent examples of this. Shopping areas often allow speedy movement into the area, but then rely on strolling and window-shopping to slow down and seduce the individual into a buying mood. Congestion is a useful aid to retail as there is excitement and interest in numbers, while it forces a slower pace. Parks will accommodate walkers, runners, cyclists and skateboarders, while often permitting motorised traffic through in certain locations as well. Water transport usually implies more measured and contemplative travel and can be one of the most pleasurable ways to experience a city. Baudelaire's *flâneur* might not be at all out of place on one of the tourist boats – the *bateaux mouches* – that every day ply the river Seine in Paris, letting people drink in the multi-sensual ambience of the city at a relaxed pace.

Neighbourhoods should always be walkable (and thus sociable) with all the necessary facilities, such as post offices, shops and schools, available within a few minutes' stroll. Much of suburbia built through the twentieth century did not provide such facilities, relying heavily upon the car. Nowadays, planning requirements enforce walkability.

↑

Name: Civic bicycle rental programme

Location: Brussels, Belgium

Date: 2009

Designer: n/a

Self-service bicycle rental kiosks have recently begun appearing in many European cities, and they serve locals and visitors alike. The bicycle is perfectly scaled to the city in terms of both speed and size.

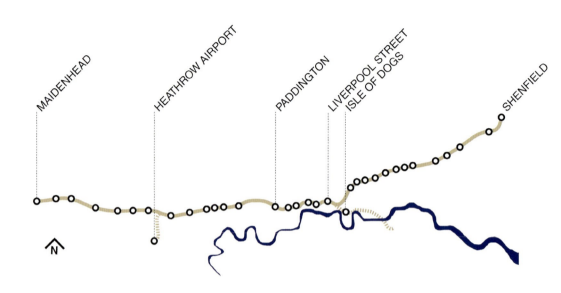

MAIDENHEAD HEATHROW AIRPORT PADDINGTON LIVERPOOL STREET ISLE OF DOGS SHENFIELD

N

←

Name: Maglev train

Location: Shanghai, China

Date: n/a

Designer: n/a

Magnetically levitating trains achieve great speed and great economy with low maintenance and low noise by eliminating friction. The cost of construction is high, however, and such schemes are easier to realise where labour costs are low.

Fast

Moving at high speeds can be exhilarating and fun, and human ambitions have always pushed the limits of possibility and experience higher, faster and longer. It is not just the thrill of speed, though, that captivates us. High-speed transportation can compress long-distance journeys into short times, allowing great opportunities for personal travel, while also bringing perishable products or time-sensitive materials to a destination sooner and fresher. High-speed links are a badge of modernity and prestige for cities, and the ambitions of an area can often be measured by the extensiveness of their state-of-the-art transportation systems. Investment in transportation infrastructure is usually seen as crucial to economic growth. London may be the exception to this rule. Although London has been the world leader in finance, it struggles with an aging transport system. Recent investment in projects such as Crossrail, a high-speed, east-west, cross-city link, may well revive prospects for the future.

High-speed transport includes not only rail transport, but also subways and other light-rail rapid transit, air travel at a variety of scales, and road-based transportation of all types from the private car to buses. Speed is, of course, relative, and a local bus is far from being as speedy or inspiring as the new magnetic levitating rail system in Shanghai.

High-speed transportation links and nodes are important to urban design as they are meeting places that tend to spur growth where they are located. It is an art to capture the vitality and vibrancy of a transport hub in a design without creating an overly sterilised environment that will all too quickly deteriorate.

←
....
Name: Crossrail diagram

Location: London, UK

Date: completion by 2017

Designer: n/a

This 118.5km rail system will span the southeast of England. Travelling in twin tunnels beneath Central London, this new rail service will provide fast connections between key transport nodes in the city.

'**Movement and change have always been part of our inheritance; static architecture has always been connected by kinetic passage – a duality echoed by life itself.**'
Lawrence Halprin

Transport modes refer to the different types of transportation, both in terms of vehicles and infrastructure, which are available for carrying passengers or cargo. When transferring from a bus to a train, for example, one is moving from the road surface to railway tracks, therefore making a change in mode.

Separation

The separation of modes of transportation involves the provision of different surfaces or lanes for different vehicle types or for pedestrians. Cycle lanes and dedicated bus lanes are prime examples of these separations. Some of these lanes might be adjacent to one another, or they might be completely at a remove. Elevated railways or country footpaths might count as two types of completely segregated tracks. Transportation modes are separated for reasons of both safety and efficiency. In rural or suburban areas, where there might be more land and wider roadways, the provision of separate lanes for transport is a matter primarily of planning, design and additional expense (that is likely to be paid back in improved health and safety). In cities, the density of occupation and movement makes separating modes extremely difficult. Many utopian schemes from the modernist era envisioned a range of solutions: from highways running at roof level to personal helicopters. While these may still be within the realm of possibility, more practical solutions have tended to be much more prosaic.

It must always be remembered that the most vulnerable transportation modes represent the bottom line for planning and design. Using this rationale, the pedestrian is the most important consideration in design for transportation. Following this would be people travelling by bicycle, skateboard, roller skates and so on. Motorcycles, cars, trucks and buses should all yield to smaller and more vulnerable modes of transportation. However, the opposite of this has generally occurred in urban settings, with pedestrians held behind railings while car traffic speeds by. Many places have tried to design out the pedestrian altogether, having no pavements at all.

Barbican Centre

↑ →

Name: The Barbican Estate – model and image

Location: London, UK

Date: 1969

Designer: Chamberlin, Powell and Bon

The Barbican was built on a site bombed during the Second World War. It fastidiously separated pedestrian traffic from vehicular traffic on raised walkways, and with underground parking and passageways.

← →
Name: Exhibition Road

Location: London, UK

Date: 2003 (in progress)

Designer: Dixon Jones Ltd

This ambitious shared-space scheme will improve pedestrian access and enliven the public realm in London's important museum district at Kensington. It will link important institutions such as the Victoria and Albert Museum and the Natural History Museum with Hyde Park and Kensington Gardens.

Shared space

Shared space is a method of designing for traffic in which the separation between different modes is abolished. Often, little or no visual distinction is made between a traditional pavement and the roadway; directional signage, pedestrian crossings and traffic signals are removed altogether. Drivers, pedestrians and other road users are thus expected to watch out for each other based upon a system of trust. At the heart of the concept is the idea that drivers and pedestrians would need to make eye contact in order to negotiate their way along the street. The principles of shared space were championed by the late Hans Mondermann of the Netherlands, and a key proponent in Britain is Ben Hamilton-Baillie, who coined the term. In places where shared space schemes have been instituted, there has been strong evidence to indicate that the number of traffic accidents falls dramatically without a significant reduction in road speeds or efficiency.

Decreased accidents and mortality would seem to be compelling arguments for using the principles of shared space, but the reality has been much more complex. Shared space may not be the correct response in all cases. Every street will have its own unique problems and solutions. Groups representing the disabled, blind or partially sighted have mounted vigorous opposition to shared space, arguing that kerbs and railings can be important navigational tools. As with all issues in urban design in the West, social and moral attitudes to sharing and caring for one another must improve in order to aid the implementation of useful design schemes. Shared space remains an important move towards mutual responsibility and community, which must surely figure as a top goal in urban design.

The futuristic dream of people gliding noiselessly through the city in individual capsules is still not a reality, nor might it ever be. Living in densely packed urban environments requires mass, usually public, transportation and alternative individual movement networks. Working out the right balance between the two increasingly requires an understanding of the multiple scales of the city, from the local to the global, and an anticipation of the fluctuating users of the space.

Individual movement

Individual movement is about choice. Choosing when to leave, which route to take and who to travel with makes individual movement systems extremely popular. The bulk of individual movement through the city is on a very local basis and is shaped by daily needs: trips to the shops and post office, exercising pets and taking children to school. In many countries, these individual journeys are made primarily on foot, though there has been, both in the developed and developing worlds, an inexorable trend towards the design of cities where the car is a necessity. Once a utopian dream advocated by architects such as Le Corbusier, many of the modernist planning projects, which only decades ago prioritised the car above the pedestrian, are being demolished and rebuilt for a pedestrian future.

While mass transport has its fixed routes and times, alternative means of travel, such as walking, cycling, or driving, usually convey the individual directly from their point of departure to their destination. They all provide door-to-door service.

It is important for urban designers to test their designs with many of these journeys as a way of refining their projects and understanding the implications.

→ ↗

Name: Bicycle Flat – images and cross-sections

Location: Amsterdam, the Netherlands

Date: 2001

Designer: VMX Architects

High population density and the overwhelming popularity of the bicycle as a mode of individual transport in Amsterdam created the need for this enormous bicycle parking garage at Central Station. It was built as a temporary structure to accommodate bicycle parking during renovations, but it may serve as a model for a more sustainable future.

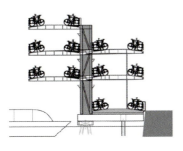

↑ →

Name: Preston Bus Station

Location: Preston, UK

Date: 1967

**Designer: Building Design
Partnership**

The remarkable bus station in
Preston is a symbol of the
modernist faith in collective
ambition and mutual support
offered by public transportation.

Movement

Name: Moscow Metro

Location: Moscow, Russia

Date: 1935

Designer: Lazar Kaganovich

Moscow's opulent metro stations prove that mass transportation needn't simply cater to the lowest common denominator, but that it can be uplifting and grand.

Mass transport

Every day in any city, large numbers of people move in, out and around, either as commuters, day trippers, or on specialised journeys.
In many places, people no longer live where they work. If each one of these journeys was made in an individual automobile, our cities would be permanently gridlocked. In reality, some of them already are. Systems and hubs for mass transportation, usually publicly funded, are required to accommodate this huge daily migration.

Mass transportation can take many forms, from the humble bus to sleek trams and underground metro systems. What all systems of mass transportation, with the exception of air travel, have in common is that they connect destinations of primary importance along primary routes. By doing so, they serve the greatest number of people. Long-distance routes, particularly trains, connect city centre to city centre, while short-distance routes, particularly those served by buses, will make connections at the neighbourhood scale.

Because of the great concentration of people and activities along mass transportation routes, and particularly at their hubs, these routes are very important to the community – they are concentrations not just of community and interaction, but of commercial and retail operations as well.

It is impossible to write a chapter about movement without acknowledging that much of what we value in cities takes place without movement at all. While we concentrate on motion, staying put is hugely important too. Urban designers must be constantly aware of the passive enjoyment of urban spaces. From waiting, to hanging out, to picnicking, or people-watching, the quality of the space must remain, even if examined closely and at length.

Resting and pausing

William Whyte's ground-breaking study, *The Social Life of Small Urban Spaces*, closely examined the ways in which people move in a public setting. He found that items, such as benches or walls for perching upon, are vital to attract people to a space. He also noted that movable seating allows people to adjust their environment to suit them, and that it puts people instantly at ease.

Staying in a place allows for meetings and exchanges to occur. People are brought together, not just in glancing blows while in motion, but through chance occurrences, such as overheard conversations or the proverbial eyes that meet across a crowded room. The room in this case could well be an urban square or a sidewalk café.

↑
Name: Mobius Bench

Location: Fukuroi City, Japan

Date: 2001

Designer: Vito Acconci

Sometimes staying still can be a tremendously dynamic experience.

→ ↓
....
Name: Paris Plage

Location: Paris, France

Date: n/a

Designer: n/a

Every year for a month in the
summer, the Georges
Pompidou expressway along
the Seine is transformed into
an urban beach – the Paris
Plage. It becomes just the
place to stop and stay for
a while.

Cities are human habitats at their most impressive and exalted. They are the physical manifestations of our dreams and aspirations, not as individuals, but as a collective. Every city is different, with flavours, textures, colours, and, of course, histories all their own. The character of a city is a combination of factors such as topography, climate and geography, but most importantly, of the people who inhabit it.

Humans shape the landscape around them and are shaped in turn by the landscape. This reciprocal relationship is at the heart of the nature of cultures, communities and urban landscapes. A city is the product of culture, but equally, it is an important shaper and creator of culture.

←
....
Name: Coming from the Mill

Location: n/a

Date: 1930

Artist: L S Lowry

Lowry became famous for painting depictions of industrial Northern England. When Lowry died in 1976, the industrial landscape that he had painted was in terminal decline; the cities of the northwest of England has spent the following decades reinventing their culture and communities with varying success.

Living together as a species on the face of the earth is a complex process, and one that is constantly changing. When trying to define the terms that frame this process, it is necessary to be purposefully vague. We all know from our personal relationships that changes accrue over time, but that they can end abruptly. Society tends to move in the same way, with long-term shifts in climate, but daily changes in weather.

Definitions

Societies are bound together by culture. Culture is a shared frame of reference that allows people within it to communicate with each other easily, and to behave well in relation to one another. It comprises collective knowledge, values and beliefs, and shapes the way a people move and strategise their way through daily life. Culture is our operating manual for the public realm.

Naturally, not everyone fits comfortably within this generalised definition. Popular music, for example, uses the chromatic scale and tends to stick to a standard time signature, but individual artists will fit within styles and genres that appeal to particular populations. Fans of the Sex Pistols may be revolted by the music of Madonna, but both employ the same musical structure. Thus, culture, once defined, must immediately be distilled into various subcultures or countercultures. The idea of 'high culture' further implies that there is a 'correct' culture to which all should aspire.

Communities, like cultures, share common values and come together for mutual support, even for survival. 'Community' is a word that has been much abused in recent decades, often used to imply a sense of camaraderie and mutual support amongst groups that might actually be at each other's throats. The dog-eat-dog world of 'the business community', for example, hardly conjures up a convivial image. It is also a community that is without a place, and thus an abstraction. It is useful for urban designers to narrow the definition of community from this rather abstract usage to specifically refer to community with propinquity – a group of people with social cohesion, who share a geographical location.

↑
....
Name: Schouwburgplein

Location: Rotterdam, Netherlands

Date: 1997

Designer: West 8

Public spaces that understand and respond to urban measures can accommodate unexpected activities.

'We prefer a world that can be modified progressively against a background of valued remains, a world in which one can leave a personal mark alongside the marks of history.' Kevin Lynch

Cities are concentrations not merely of human populations, but also of political, cultural, societal and economic institutions. The exercise of earthly power and the accumulation and expenditure of great wealth are hallmarks of city life.

Power and money

The Greek word for city is *polis*, a word which is at the heart of the term 'politics'. Politics can describe either the process of government or the complex interrelationships between people living together in a community. Politics, though, is underscored with connotations of power and wealth, and the exercise (and abuse) of both.

Landscapes often speak explicitly of power. Louis XIV's gardens at Versailles are a clear statement of dominion over not just people, but nature, too. Many city spaces were created not for the public good, but rather to impress upon the populace the supreme power of either government or religion. The Forbidden City in Beijing is a good example of this, with a clear hierarchy of spaces accessible only to a select few. All of Beijing was planned as a great capital city from the beginning. In the 1950s and 1960s, planners under Mao Zedong orchestrated the demolition of Beijing's massive, majestic city walls to replace them with transportation infrastructure, and there was also major clearance to create the enormous Tiananmen Square. Tiananmen Square might be considered the opposite of a public space. Its totalitarian scale dwarfs the individual and forces them to feel subservient to the power of the state. It is a space best suited to parading troops and weaponry, not to active citizen participation in the daily life of a metropolis.

Nowadays, relatively few public spaces are created with only the public good in mind. More often than not, urban spaces are viewed from a more corporate viewpoint that sees only their economic value. Even trees must now be given a cash value for people to gauge the importance of keeping them. Urban designers must be constantly vigilant to ensure that the functions of public squares are not given over totally to commerce or to flashy spectacles that have little to do with the pleasant banality of everyday life.

→ ↘

Name: Shanghai Masterplan – diagram and model

Location: Shanghai, China

Date: 1994

Designer: Rogers, Stirk, Harbour + Partners

The grand radiating boulevards of the Shanghai Masterplan are representative of urban form that is only possible with the concentration of political power characteristic of an authoritarian state. The Richard Rogers masterplan has managed to introduce civic aspirations in this rigid plan, incorporating an ambitious park and a comprehensive public transportation system.

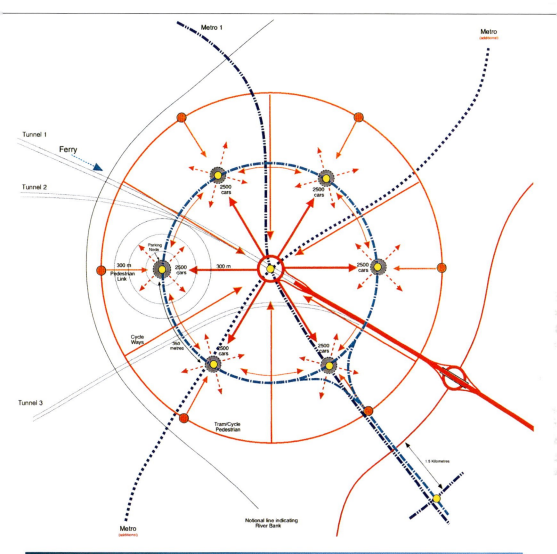

Metro 1

Metro
(additional)

Tunnel 1

Ferry

Tunnel 2

2500
cars

2500
cars

Parking
Node

300 m

2500
cars

300 m

2500
cars

Pedestrian
Link

Cycle
Ways

350
metres

2500
cars

2500
cars

Tunnel 3

Tram/Cycle
Pedestrian

1·5 Kilometres

Metro
(additional)

Notional line indicating
River Bank

Public and private

Urban design work undertaken by landscape architects is perhaps most commonly public work. At scales from the neighbourhood to city-wide this is almost always true, but increasingly the lines between what is public and what is private are blurred. For example, private security guards at Paddington Basin in London ensure that members of the public do not linger or take photographs on what appear to be public streets. City government has abdicated its stewardship of the public realm in exchange for private investment, resulting in a private police force.

Shopping malls have been a more traditional battleground between public and private interests, with shops organised along indoor 'streets' that are clearly not public, and where behaviour may be rigorously policed. The democratic function of true public spaces allows for the exchange of ideas and the coexistence of people from all walks of life. The more that private interests shield people from public discourse, the less real freedom anyone has.

The terminology used to discuss the public areas of a city is often confused and ambiguous, crossing disciplinary borders between architecture, planning, geography, politics and sociology, amongst other fields. The 'public realm' is a common term within landscape discourse, and in urban design terms it generally refers to any areas where people may freely meet. The 1748 Giambattista Nolli Map of Rome (known as the Nolli Map) shows streets and squares as voids, but also interior spaces, such as churches and civic buildings. Private spaces, such as homes and businesses, are shown as opaque masses. All of these spaces we would know today as the public realm. 'Public domain' and 'public sphere' generally refer to the world of ideas, and do not specifically refer to public space.

Finally, there are gradations between public and private. Often, spaces are described as 'semi-public' or 'semi-private', and this refers to spaces that are open, at least to a majority of the public, such as railway stations, shops and cafés. Usually, the implication is that all are welcome, as long as they are able to pay.

→

Name: Canary Wharf Masterplan

Location: London, UK

Date: 1993

Designer: Skidmore, Owings and Merrill

The lifeless and sanitised streets and squares of Canary Wharf are heavily policed and scrupulously cleansed, but lack the public spirit and healthy exchange of a public city.

The minority

Public space holds particular importance for many different types of minorities, for whom a certain amount of visibility might be crucial to survival. There are many different types of minorities, ranging from subcultural and countercultural elements (including political dissidents) to racial and ethnic minorities, the disabled, various religions, gays and lesbians, both the young and the old, and the poor and disadvantaged.

Each of these minorities will use the city in different ways, and often they will colonise urban space. These groups may either actively migrate to certain areas, as with artists to New York's Brooklyn (or London's Soho), or they may be forced through social, economic or legal pressure into certain areas in a process of ghettoisation, as Blacks were forced into Harlem, or the Chinese into Chinatown, in the same city.

Contemporary economic and political systems worldwide tend to favour the uneven distribution of wealth and opportunity, and until a solution is found to this imbalance, cities will naturally stratify into richer and poorer areas, undergoing boom and bust cycles of deterioration and regeneration.

→

Name: *Hollow Land*

Location: Occupied territories

Date: 2007

Designer: Eyal Weizman

Hollow Land is a fascinating exploration of the political space created by Israel's occupation of Gaza and the West Bank. The work examines the transformation of the landscape through the total control of space, from the subterranean to the militarised airspace.

←
....
Name: Alphaville

Location: São Paolo, Brazil

Date: 1974

Designer: Alphaville Urbanismo S A

The violent reputation of São Paolo's urban streets has led many of the city's wealthier inhabitants to shelter in gated enclaves such as Alphaville. Ironically named after Jean-Luc Godard's dystopic film of the same name, it bristles with cameras, alarms and security that guard an improbable landscape.

Ghettos and gated communities

Segregation, whether enforced or chosen, has always been a fact of life in cities. A ghetto is generally understood to be an impoverished and usually ethnic area of a city. People here live not only together for mutual survival and defence, but also for the support of a shared language and culture. Ghettos have also been enforced through history as a way of segregating an undesired population.

Ironically, the wealthy also often choose to segregate themselves in gated communities. These defensive compounds within the city protect them from the perceived or real dangers of the world outside. Neither ghettos nor gated communities do much to serve mutual understanding and coexistence in genuinely democratic places.

Civic life is formed by the complex interaction between individuals and society in urban space. Manners are our code for civic behaviour, and they differ from culture to culture and from city to city. Cultural expectations about how we use space have great impact on the design of spaces, especially at the scale of the neighbourhood, the street and the public square.

Neighbourhoods

A neighbourhood is often what defines the physical reach of a community. Generally speaking, it is at a walkable scale, with shops and facilities, and a distinct identity. Often, neighbourhoods will have a name, but sometimes, as in New York, they might be defined by only a couple of city blocks, or even by the length of a street. Sometimes, a neighbourhood will have a name that takes on what used to exist where it was built, such as 'The Meadows' or 'Deer Run'.

Neighbourhoods are the imprint of a community upon urban space, and they take time and occupation to grow and establish themselves. Good urban design will allow for incremental change, as well as flexibility of use in structures. The design of housing at Borneo-Sporenburg in Amsterdam, for example, has allowed for the conversion of the ground floor of houses to small-scale commercial uses, reflecting the Dutch tradition of individual enterprise. This is in spite of the development's zoning, which at present prohibits this use. It is a healthy recognition that the design of urban spaces must allow for flexibility to ensure that they have a future.

Often, one of the great problems with large, glitzy developments is that the whole deteriorates on the same schedule. Huge maintenance bills pile up all at once and cannot be paid. Thus, the young professionals who move into a sparkling complex may be trapped in old age in a ruined landscape ruled by crime and poverty. We all like to think that our mobility will allow escape, but times, situations and means are always changing. A healthy neighbourhood allows for change.

↑
....

Name: Bo01

Location: Malmö, Sweden

Date: 2001

Designer: Various architects

Bo01 is an ambitious housing development that not only integrates energy production and passive solar design, but also aims to meet the requirements of a sustainable community.

Meeting places and social spaces

A successful neighbourhood relies on the accumulated goodwill created by chance meetings and encounters with familiar faces on a daily basis. The atmosphere of trust that emerges makes a neighbourhood feel safe and friendly. Much of this happens naturally, but it is certainly possible to design spaces that prevent or impede this from developing. Great, windswept spaces that make people into tiny figures on a horizon, or tight uncomfortable spaces that force people to scurry through without making eye contact, are ways to ruin the chances of community development through bad design. It is relatively easy to design spaces that bring people together to create warmth and conviviality.

The town square is probably the most important public space of all. It is usually centrally located, but in many port cities, it may be located on the waterfront. The town square is not only a social space, but a place for festivals, events, speeches and pageantry; it provides civic and cultural cohesion for a whole city – not just neighbourhoods. Aside from a main town square, neighbourhoods are often organised around squares of their own, which are often heavily used by locals for gathering, playing, exercising, or simply relaxing. Many areas are animated by markets, which provide important spaces not just for commerce, but for all types of civic exchange.

Promenades and the public street perform the important function of channelling people past one another, providing the opportunity for meeting and recognition. Finally, parks perform an important function not just as ecological spaces (the 'green lungs' of the city), but also contain important pedestrian links through the urban fabric, as well as multiple opportunities for healthful recreation.

It should be stressed that all of the spaces described above have their greatest importance to community and civic identity as pedestrian spaces – a design that favours the car tends to devalue the rest.

→
Name: Borough Market

Location: London, UK

Date: n/a

Designer: n/a

Borough Market exists as a community of traders and tenants. It is also a focal point for local communities, businesses and visitors.

→
Name: Invalidenpark

Location: Berlin, Germany

Date: 1997

Designer: Atelier Girot

This image depicts a moment of pleasant isolation and contemplation at Christoph Girot's celebrated Invalidenpark. The 'sinking wall' in the fountain is a direct reference to the Berlin wall, itself a symbol of isolation, separation and alienation in the city.

Anonymity and isolation

A great irony of city life is that amidst the teeming masses, cities can be lonely places. The great numbers of people often make it impossible to greet people or exchange pleasantries. Many people find cities to be desperately isolating and depressing places. Alienation often occurs when people are unable to find personal meaning in their urban environment. Design can go some way towards mitigating this problem, but it is also an issue of the management and administration of public spaces. People need to feel that they have a stake in the spaces around them. Often, this can be achieved with as little as the provision of seating, but it commonly involves much more complex negotiations. Alienation leads people to feel they have no control over their environment; this is often the case when management is neglectful or disinterested, or when administration of spaces is too heavy handed. Community consultation can exacerbate matters if people are asked for advice and then ignored. This only magnifies the sense of powerlessness.

Anonymity on the other hand, rather than alienation, can actually be a comfort; people speak of the pleasure of 'losing one's self in a crowd'. Small town or rural living can be stifling to those who resent the intrusion of others – though of course, this same 'intrusion' also goes toward defining a sense of community. People often feel the need to reinvent themselves, and the city offers plenty of possibility to leave an old identity behind.

Human necessities at the personal scale include food, shelter and sleep. Human populations have more complex requirements, but the essence of these are similar. Cities should be safe, healthy and good environments in which to learn and grow.

Education and health

Central to the construction of viable neighbourhoods is the availability and proximity of educational and health services. Healthy bodies and minds are crucial to happiness and well-being. Good neighbourhood day care facilities, kindergartens and primary schools are an important part of ensuring that children are properly socialised, and that their associations allow them the freedom of their local streets amongst people they know and who know them. Secondary schools may be located further afield, with students relying on foot power, public transportation or bicycles to travel to and from school. Secondary schools should ideally be local and of good quality in all neighbourhoods, rich or poor.

Education is also important for providing instruction in civics, teaching people how to act and behave in public, and showing them how they can make good, informed use of the spaces that are designed for them. Education in civics can range from how to cross a road and on which side of the sidewalk to walk, to more complex issues involving the politics of space and each individual's right to community and political engagement.

People also need access to local doctors and dentists, and they should have good hospitals and ambulance services that are within easy reach by public transportation. A crucial element of public health is ensuring that all people have access to quality public spaces, especially parks and sporting facilities, so that they may actively engage in an outdoor life that contributes to wellness and well-being.

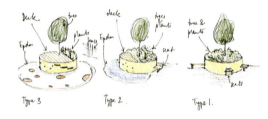

→ ↘

Name: University of Michigan Masterplan

Location: Ann Arbor, USA

Date: 1997

Designer: Venturi, Scott Brown and Associates

The University of Michigan Masterplan takes a very long view – over 100 years – of the future growth of the university and of its relationship to the civic life of the whole town of Ann Arbor. The university presently has campuses distributed throughout the area, which creates challenges for unifying the campus. It also provides opportunities to link the life of the mind with the life of the town.

← ↙

Name: Golden Lane Campus

Location: London, UK

Date: 2008

Designer: Farrer Huxley Associates

This exceptionally sensitive primary school campus design maximises rooftop space and provides for imaginative play for children in London's most dense core.

OPTIONS FOR AN ARTS SCIENCE AXIS

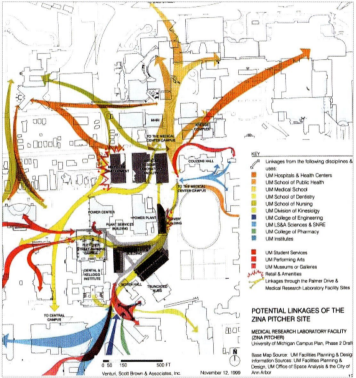

POTENTIAL LINKAGES OF THE ZINA PITCHER SITE

MEDICAL RESEARCH LABORATORY FACILITY (ZINA PITCHER)
University of Michigan Campus Plan, Phase 2 Draft

Base Map Source: UM Facilities Planning & Design
Information Sources: UM Facilities Planning &
Design, UM Office of Space Analysis & the City of
Ann Arbor

Venturi, Scott Brown & Associates, Inc.   November 12, 1999

Public safety

If any city is to be successful, it must be safe. Cities that fail to provide safe environments can become nightmarish and dysfunctional, as evidenced by the cities of São Paulo in Brazil and Johannesburg in South Africa. Huge private investment has been made in creating fortified homes and suburbs, and efforts at public safety have simply been abandoned in many areas. Though advances in public safety have been made in both cities in the last decade or so, the economic collapse of the late 2000s could well threaten these efforts.

The fortress approach is only one way of ensuring safety, and it is usually the last resort. No one wants to live in a neighbourhood where businesses operate from behind shutters and bars. Regulation is the most common approach, with physical policing forming the backbone of public safety efforts. Surveillance is also often employed, with countries such as the United Kingdom constantly monitoring almost every centimetre of urban public space. The effectiveness of electronic surveillance is much debated, however, and there are serious issues with infringements on civil liberties.

Urban designers can do much to assist with the security of public spaces by providing good lighting and clear sight lines, for example. There is great value to what is known as natural surveillance, or 'eyes on the street', where buildings front onto the public realm and blank facades without windows are avoided. Street networks should avoid dead ends and culs-de-sac and strive for a more open network.

Good relationships between buildings and their contexts also help to ensure that people feel a sense of ownership over the space around them.

Designers can do much to avoid crime and improve public safety, but it is still crucial for local governments to think holistically about supporting design with other reforms, in particular, fighting poverty and inequality.

↑

Name: CCTV and street art

Location: London, UK

Date: n/a

Designer: Banksy

The pervasive nature of CCTV in London is challenged by street artist, Banksy.

General approaches to providing public safety in urban spaces

The fortress: This method uses shutters, gates, and barbed wire to create an enclosure that keeps crime at bay. This method creates an environment that looks dangerous and crime-ridden.

The panoptic: This could take the impersonal form of security cameras, which make spaces feel unsafe even if they are not. Areas such as windows, porches or busy walkways provide 'eyes on the street' as they are always in view of people.

The regulatory: This refers to signage or the physical presence of police or wardens.
Good signage combined with appropriate and sensitive community policing can help make a neighbourhood feel very secure.

The informal sector and informal settlement

In any country, particularly in developing countries, a certain portion of the market will be untaxed or untaxable, existing outside of formal shops and markets. This may be damaging or dangerous, such as in the case of the black market trade in smuggled or contraband goods, or it may be as benign as a traditional barter system in which goods are traded fairly amongst individuals without the exchange of cash. 'Freecycling', where unwanted goods are simply given away, might also be classed as part of the informal sector. The informal sector can have a huge impact upon the character and the physical expression of an area. In London's Soho, for example, the informal sex trade is considered by many small local businesses to be crucial to keeping rents low enough for them to survive and to keep out the large chain stores. Here, the sex trade also serves as an attraction for tourists who come innocently enough to photograph the neon and the marquees.

The informal sector has its equivalent in the built forms of many cities. Often, pressures for housing are so great that formal regulating agencies cannot stay ahead of demand, or cannot enforce land-use planning measures. This can result in the growth of slums or *favelas* that are often without basic services such as roads and sewerage. Sometimes, though, informal settlement may be a political act, as with political communes or some squatter settlements. Christiania, near Copenhagen in Denmark, was a collective and semi-legal, self-governing community established in the early 1970s; it is perhaps the most famous example of an informal, autonomous settlement. In 2004, it was officially abolished by the Danish government, but controversy and protests continue to occur. After all, how does one officially abolish something that was never official to begin with?

→

Name: Slums in Kroo Bay

Location: Freetown, Liberia

Date: n/a

Designer: n/a

For many years, economic development has privileged the city and forced people off the land. This has put huge strain on urban housing in many places and often informal slums such as this are people's only solution for shelter.

←

Name: Elephant and Castle

Location: London, UK

Date: n/a

Designer: n/a

The public spaces of Elephant and Castle currently provide a setting for informal activities and architectures.

Cities are unparalleled for providing welcome distractions and thrilling spectacles. From great events requiring years of preparation, such as the 2008 Olympic and Paralympic Games in Beijing, to tourist destinations that may have required hundreds of years of cilivisation to develop, diversions are part of the urban experience.

Entertainment and sports

Urban areas have always provided a great concentration of entertainment and diversion, whether simple people-watching or giant spectacles. The 2008 Olympic and Paralympic Games in Beijing may have been one of the most elaborate spectacles the world will ever see, and its impact upon Beijing's urban form has been profound. Increasingly, though, it seems people now expect to be entertained rather than to find ways to entertain themselves. Cities are themselves a playground, a source of endless fascination. Guy Debord, in *The Society of the Spectacle,* claimed that good citizens should lead lives of action and invention, rather than of leisure and consumption.[1] The forces of the market rather militate against this, however.

↑

Name: PS1

Location: Long Island City, USA

Date: 2008

Designer: n/a

Founded in 1971, PS1 is a contemporary arts organisation that is now an affiliate of the Museum of Modern Art (MoMA). Their annual 'Warm Up' series of music events attracts a diverse community of music fans, artists and families alike.

1. Debord, Guy. *The Society of the Spectacle.* Rebel Press, London, 1992 (originally published 1967).

←
....
**Name: The O$_2$ Centre
(formerly known as the
Millennium Dome)**

Location: London, UK

Date: 1999

**Designer: Rogers Stirk
Harbour and Partners**

Often, the perceived need for a
city to create a spectacle as an
economic engine can go
dreadfully wrong. A combination
of media wrath, public enmity
and resentment helped to
ensure the failure of the
Millennium Dome – a giant,
fabric building filled with
multimedia displays. It has been
reinvented as a large-events
venue and has since been
more successful.

Shopping

Shopping started off as an innocent enough
activity. Basic household goods, food and
clothing all need to be produced and acquired,
and few homes are self-sufficient.
Industrialisation centralised the facilities that
produced these goods, and thus, commerce in
such goods also became centralised. It was
only a matter of time before companies went
from simply selling people things they needed
to finding ways to extract money in exchange
for products that were completely unnecessary.
In the process, both shopping and branding
have become huge industries, champions of
leisure and consumption. Corporate shopping
has utterly transformed the fabric of the city,
making all places a bit more familiar and a bit
more generic, with the same brands appearing
worldwide. This comes at a cost to local and
cultural identity. Shopping is easy
entertainment, but it is far from free.

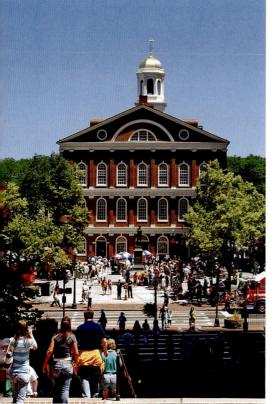

←
....
**Name: Faneuil Hall urban
renewal project**

Location: Boston, USA

Date: 1976

**Designer: Benjamin
Thompson and Jim Rouse
(developer)**

The reinvention of Boston's
once-dilapidated Faneuil Hall
and the associated Quincy
Market was a first in the
adaptive reuse of historic
buildings as shopping and
tourist destinations. Its huge
commercial success has since
inspired many imitators.

Tourism

Tourism has had a profound impact upon the shape and presentation of many cities. In centuries past, if people travelled at all, they may only have made one big trip in their entire lives. Advances in transportation technology through the twentieth century have made the world a progressively smaller place. What was once only accessible through books and the imagination now appears right on our doorsteps, or at least only a short flight away. Tourism has proven a real cash cow for many places that are long on scenery, but short on other resources. It has also been an additional boon for places that have built inspiring cities because of superior resources.

Tourism has also been an invaluable tool in preservation, allowing people to value their heritage. Still, there are tensions. Are popular tourist cities becoming pickled and inflexible? Have they had their progress stunted by trying to live up to the expectations of tourists? Mass tourism, such as package tours, tends to devalue local cultures and can be a serious strain on fragile environments. On the other hand, eco and cultural tourism, which often consists of small groups travelling to see the 'real' culture of a place, can be of exceptional value for preservation.

↙ ←

Name: Landscape and sculpture in Lanzarote

Location: Canary Islands, Spain

Date: 1960s and 1970s

Designer: César Manrique

Manrique was creative in many arts, including architecture and urban design. He transformed his native island into a self-consciously sculpted holiday paradise. Urban design for tourism often seeks to work with existing cities, but it can also create destinations from scratch.

Clandestine

The informal sector has spawned many uses for urban space, from the subversive to the illegal. Many such uses are exactly what Guy Debord had in mind when he spoke of action and invention. These uses might range from the spectacular funambulism of Philippe Petit on a high wire strung between the twin towers of New York's World Trade Center, to raves and house parties. Many involve the thrill of danger or transgression, and others are simply wanton acts of destruction. However, many such acts embody important methods of urban reinvention, sowing the seeds for the urban future.

←

Name: Southbank Centre

Location: London, UK

Date: 1967

Designer: Hubert Bennett (Greater London Council) with Jack Whittle, F G West and Geoffrey Horsefall

In recent years, the unused understorey spaces of the Southbank's Queen Elizabeth Hall have evolved to become a focus for graffiti and skating. The attraction of these activities for viewing tourists has contributed to the tolerance of them by the authorities and the police.

The themes of this book – context, measure, movement, community and culture – may all be seen as dynamic systems and interdependent factors that interact in the work of urban design. These factors are in action before the designer comes to a site and they continue after the packing up of the last contractor, the cutting of the ribbon and the uncorking of the champagne.

Both urban design and the city itself are processes over time and at various scales. While a project occurs within a given time frame and at a predetermined scale, it is simultaneously influenced by and reaches out to many other landscape scales, across the continuum of time. The project is always under the processes of change, adaptation and reinvention. These happen over many layers of time. The following case studies allow us to understand in more detail the potential discourse between landscape architecture, urban design, and the built and natural environments of the city.

←
....
Name: Ancoats Public Realm Strategy

Location: Manchester, UK

Date: 2009

Designer: Camlin Lonsdale

The Ancoats Public Realm Strategy was commissioned to inform and guide future development of the Ancoats Urban Village.

Urban design projects can provide essential structure for the future city. Many of these structures will manifest themselves physically in the plan of a city. The following three projects represent a diversity of approaches, including the design of both physical space and guidelines or 'rules' for that space, which provide a unique context for future buildings, open space and interventions.

Name: Borneo Sporenburg

Location: Amsterdam, Netherlands

Date: 1993

Designer: West 8

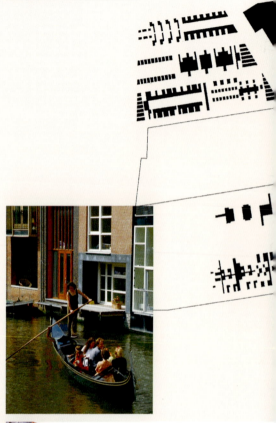

Case study: Borneo Sporenburg

Borneo Sporenburg is a mixed-use development located on two industrial peninsulas in the Amsterdam Docks. In 1993, the Dutch firm West 8 was commissioned to prepare a masterplan that delivered a density of 100 dwelling units per hectare. Their proposal included new residential typologies based on the traditional Dutch canal house, adapting the form for a new urban setting. Over 100 different architects were then commissioned to design the individual houses. A public, open-space infrastructure was set out to provide bridges, parks and circulation space to connect the two peninsulas. This network of open space has become an essential component of the design, providing public presence while contrasting with the individuality of the private houses.

The plan provides a distinctive design that balances repetition with individuality. The field of three-storey dwelling units creates a consistent image of the development, punctuated by three large apartment buildings. These add to the residential density and allow a greater range of tenants at different income levels.

Discussion point:

[1] Challenging established building typologies was key to the masterplan for Borneo Sporenburg. Could new landscape typologies establish frameworks for future urban design projects?

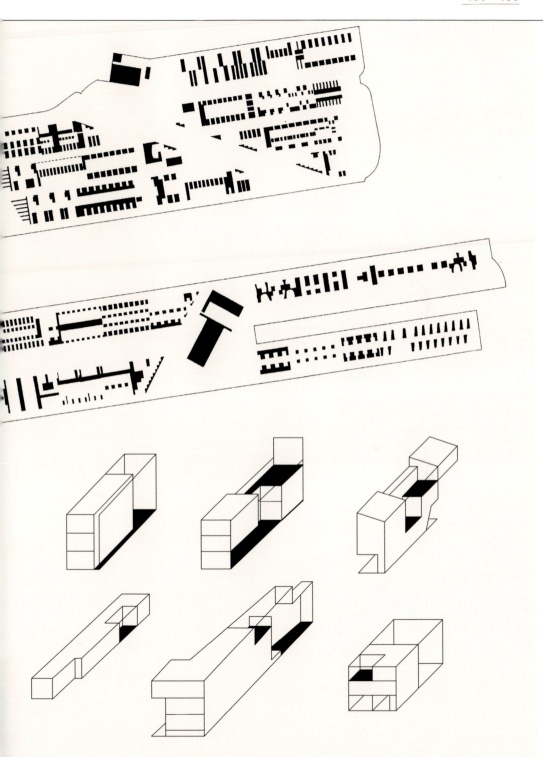

Case study: Ancoats

In the late 1700s, a network of streets was laid out in Ancoats to create a new industrial district in Manchester. Argued to be the world's first industrial suburb, Ancoats was transformed from a hamlet of cottages to a gridiron plan of warehouses that was serviced by the Rochdale Canal. Due to the rapid growth of the cotton industry, the area became densely developed with warehouses and cramped terrace housing, but it was devoid of any open space.

The industrial growth of northwest England fluctuated for the next 200 years. However, from the end of the Second World War Ancoats was in terminal decline. In the 1990s, due to its industrial heritage, the site was designated a conservation area, and a regeneration company was formed to manage its redevelopment. Ancoats Urban Village Company commissioned Camlin Lonsdale to set out and implement a strategy for the public realm. A new public infrastructure was to lead the regeneration of Ancoats, creating a strong framework for any future development. The strategic approach taken by Camlin Lonsdale included identifying a street hierarchy and simplifying the existing circulation patterns. As with many shared-space projects, different techniques were employed to promote a pedestrian-led public realm, which reduced the speed of traffic by removing the 'rules' for navigating the streets.

Two public spaces have created moments of distinction within the consistent Ancoats street pattern. A canal-side square opens up the public realm to the important canal infrastructure, and a new public square sits within the street grid where industrial buildings once stood. As the development of Ancoats continues, the robust design developed by Camlin Lonsdale should be able to attract and accommodate the changes that will occur, allowing for the long-term reuse of this unique district of industrial Manchester.

↑ →

Name: Ancoats Public Realm Strategy

Location: Manchester, UK

Date: 2009

Designer: Camlin Lonsdale

Discussion point:

[1] The ability to consider diverse scales, movement and processes of change through time make some landscape architects ideally suited for complex urban projects. It is therefore important to consider the diversity of skills needed to inform each individual project.

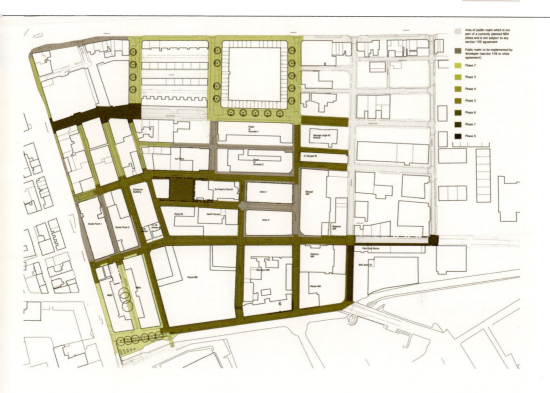

Case study: Eixample

Ildefons Cerdà is most famous for the design of the gridiron street plan of Barcelona. The project, Eixample, was a comprehensive and modern extension of Barcelona, incorporating pedestrians, carriages, trams and urban railways, along with utilities of gas and sanitation.

Cerdà originally trained as a civil engineer and was commissioned to develop the extension plan of Barcelona by the Spanish central government, with the support of the city council. When he was unable to find a suitable precedent for the project, he developed his own methodology by borrowing technological ideas to create a fully integrated city system.

The plan is characterised by the orthogonal grid that colonised the territory beyond the traditional walled city. While suggesting a simple occupation of agricultural land, the plan was sophisticated and complex in its responsiveness to the anticipated movement systems and the integration with historic routes. Each city block was designed with chamfered edges and was to include a central garden area. Two striking axes were proposed to cut through the grid towards the sea – one reaching the historic district of Barceloneta, and the other extending to the site of the present day Barcelona Forum.

While the Eixample, commonly known as the Cerdà Plan, has come to define the ambition of Barcelona's urbanism, it courted controversy at the time. The existing landowners were unhappy with the proposed subdivision of the Barcelona territory, while many local architects accused Cerdà of promoting socialism. Fortunately, however, the main elements of Cerdà's plan were approved by the government and have provided a unique framework for the generations of architects and urban designers who have worked in the Catalan capital.

Discussion point:

[1] Which ideas will inform the future city? Urban design and landscape architecture must regularly look not only within their own theory and practice, but to other disciplines to generate new concepts for forms, processes and systems.

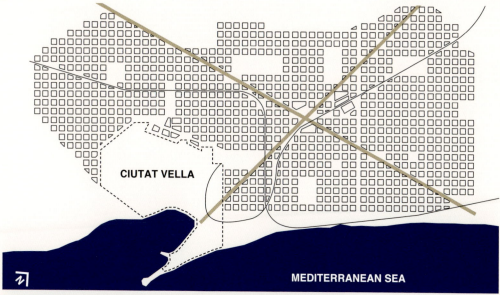

CIUTAT VELLA

MEDITERRANEAN SEA

←↑

Name: Eixample (Cerdà Plan)

Location: Barcelona, Spain

Date: 1859

Designer: Ildefons Cerdà

The simplicity of a line belies the complexity of the movement systems that it can represent. The following projects reveal a diversity of solutions to situations of movement. Some attempt to create complex scenarios within their design, while others rationalise already elaborate movement systems. All the projects demonstrate movement across the landscape and the potential of movement as a strategic urban design project.

Case study: Barceloneta

Barceloneta is one of the neighbourhoods in Barcelona that pre-dates the Cerdà Plan. The area is composed of a triangular peninsula that projects into the sea and was originally the home to residents displaced from the Ribera neighbourhood. Barceloneta is now enclosed by the Mediterranean Sea, Port Vell and the El Born neighbourhood, and is renowned for its restaurants and nightclubs.

The historic buildings of Barceloneta are mainly arranged on long thin blocks that are only one building wide. This grid of streets sits at 45 degrees to the sea and the Barceloneta Seaside Promenade, designed in 1998 by the Barcelona City Council. While the buildings have been renovated for predominantly private uses, the public realm is structured around the beach with a linear walkway that rises up from the level of the beach to 7.4m above sea level. The change in level allows for an upper promenade, which connects with the existing city, to cantilever over a lower promenade that connects with the beach. The new space under the cantilever is occupied by restaurants, sports facilities and service rooms for the lifeguards, creating an active seam along the city's water edge.

The Barceloneta Seaside Promenade follows previous projects since the 1980s, which have re-orientated the city of Barcelona towards the sea. Through land-use changes and movement projects, such as extending existing boulevards and connecting existing thoroughfares, the formerly industrial waterfront has been transformed, reinventing the image of the city.

Discussion point:
[1] Large urban projects must consider the functional use of the city, but what should these functions be? Should they be public or private? Exclusive or inclusive? Structured or informal?

↗ →
....
Name: Plaça del Mar, New Seaside Promenade of Barceloneta

Location: Barcelona, Spain

Date: 1996

Designer: Jordi Henrich, Olga Tarrasó, Jaume Artigues, Miquel Roig, Barcelona City Council Urban Projects Service

BARCELONETA

MEDITERRAN

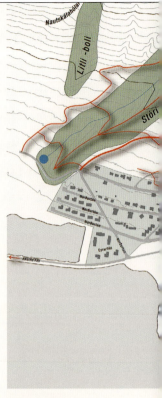

Case study: Avalanche barriers

In 1997, the engineering firm Hnit were commissioned to lead the design of avalanche barriers at Siglufjordur, North Iceland. Hnit worked closely with the landscape architects at Landslag to realise linear landforms that would protect the town. The larger barrier below Ytra Strengsgil is 700m long and 18m high, while the smaller landform is a third of the length but still reaches 15m in height.

Although modelled from 329 000m^3 of material, the sinuous barriers have assimilated with the existing mountain landscape while also referencing the creative landforms of many environmental artists. The avalanche barriers work with the natural ecosystems of the Icelandic landscape while also possessing essential urban qualities. This recognition was highlighted when Landslag received a special mention in the Rosa Barba European Landscape Prize for the theme of 'Only with Nature'.

Discussion point:
[1] Projects that look to the processes of the landscape for inspiration can appreciate the context of diverse ecosystems. How can these begin to inform the built forms of the city?

↑ →
....
Name: Avalanche barriers

Location: Siglufjördur, Iceland

Date: 1999

Designer: Hnit and Landslag

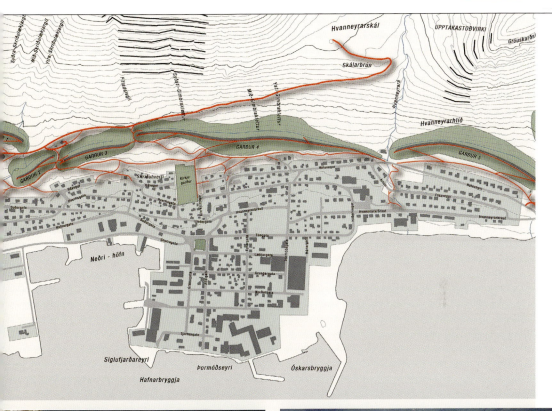

Síðra-Skríðuklettagil Mið-Skríðuklettagil Ytra-Skríðuklettagil
Hvanneyrarskál
UPPTAKASTÖÐVIRKI
Gróuskarðsá
Skálarbrún
Finnbogagil
Síðsti-Gimbraklettur
Mið-Gimbraklettur
Ýsti-Gimbraklettur
Hvanneyrará
Hvanneyrarhlíð
GARÐUR 3
GARÐUR 4
GARÐUR 5
GARÐUR 2
Skríðuhverfi
Kirkju garður
Hólavegur
Háavegur
Hverfisgata
Hólavegur
Hverfisgata
Hverfisgata
Fossvegur
Suðurgata
Grundargata
Laugarvegur
Hvanneyrarbraut
Hvanneyrarbraut
Hvanneyrarbraut
Aðalgata
Hólavegur
Hafnargata
Neðri - höfn
Hvanneyrarbraut
Gránugata
Aðalgata
Vetrarbraut
Túngata
Eyrargata
Lækjargata
Hafnargata
Grundargata
Norðurgata
Tjarnargata
Siglufjarðareyri
Þormóðseyri
Óskarsbryggja
Hafnarbryggja

Projects and processes

← Structure **Lines** Points →

↑ ← ↙
Name: The Highline

Location: New York, USA

Date: 2009

Designer: Field Operations
with Diller Scofidio + Renfro

Case study: The High Line

The High Line is a steel and concrete elevated railway built in 1934, spanning 22 city blocks between 34th Street and Gansevoort Street in New York City. The structure was originally designed to carry freight trains between certain buildings and locations along the west side of Manhattan. As with much of the railway infrastructure in the United States, the High Line became increasingly less used until the last train operated on the structure in the 1980s.

In 1999, a group called 'Friends of the High Line' formed to advocate the preservation and reuse of the structure. They were joined in 2002 by groups of business owners, who recognised the potential that the High Line offered for the area. This growing lobby of diverse interests was inspired by the Promenade Plantée in Paris, a reused railway structure that has now become a popular city park.

In 2009, the first stage of the High Line reconstruction was opened with great interest from local residents, businesses and designers. The High Line is the first major project completed by the landscape architects Field Operations, and is a project often cited by landscape urbanism advocates. The High Line project incorporates urban ecological analysis to create a park space designed for a diversity of new functions. The design team, composed of Diller Scofidio and Renfro Architects, Olafur Eliasson, Piet Oudolf, and Buro Happold, has also provided a powerful vision for the space, attracting a high project profile with advocates from politics, culture, business and entertainment. While the park will foster new perspectives of the city, the project has already enhanced the dialogue between landscape architecture and urban design.

Discussion point:

[1] Realising theoretical speculations in built form has been the preoccupation of many great landscape architects. How can concepts and theories retain their integrity through often difficult project processes?

Case study: Euralille

The Euralille project began with the initiative to position the former industrial city of Lille as a new business centre. At the strategic intersection of the new TGV–Eurostar high-speed rail connections to London, Paris and Brussels, Lille was to become a new crossroads that would change the way Europe was experienced and perceived.

Rem Koolhaas and his Office for Metropolitan Architecture were commissioned in 1988 to design a vast masterplan for an area that would bring together the new Gare TGV Lille Europe Station and the old Lille Flandres train station. The masterplan area covered 120 acres of central Lille with four main elements: the Triangle des Gares, the international train station, a park and the Grand Palais. Within this structure, the programme for the buildings included shopping, offices, parking, transport, hotels, housing, concert hall and congress accommodation funded by both private and public interests.

The vast scale of the development and the potential for large flows of people passing through this new European centre are reminiscent of contemporary airports. Although adjacent to the historic city, this modern development aims to accommodate unique contemporary activities, increasing the complexity of the experience of arriving, departing or passing through.

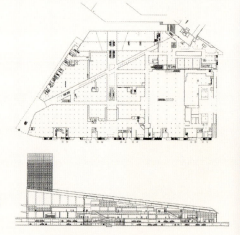

↑ →

Name: Euralille Master Plan

Location: Lille, France

Date: 1994

Designer: Office for Metropolitan Architecture

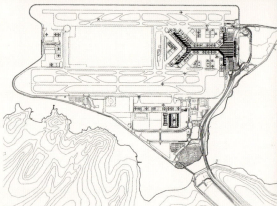

Discussion points:

[1] Can large-scale infrastructure be reconciled with historic urban centres?

[2] What qualities are created, destroyed or emerge from these impositions on the city landscape?

← ↑

Name: Chek Lap Kok

Location: Hong Kong, China

Date: 1998

Designer: Foster + Partners

Case study: Chek Lap Kok

The design of Stansted Airport outside of London marked a departure in the design of airports. Two main concepts were incorporated into the design. First, the airport was to recapture the simplicity of early airports where there was a linear, visual and physical route from land side to air side. This approach was facilitated by the second concept of taking many of the traditional functions of the airport and moving them from the ceiling to beneath the concourse floor. With the completion of this work by Norman Foster in 1991, these concepts have since been developed further in the design of Hong Kong's Chek Lap Kok airport.

Chek Lap Kok is the name of one of the two islands that were flattened and merged to create the site for this massive airport. This action created a tabula rasa for the new airport, presenting the traveller with views of the sea and shops lit with natural light. Like Euralille, the new airport required a vast space dictated by large transport infrastructures. Both projects also represent a changing view on the global experience, and a grappling with the concept of what the French anthropologist Marc Augé, calls 'non-place'. These spaces of transience – such as hotels, airports and supermarkets – lack the uniqueness of context that would give them individual identity. As urban design projects, they exist as processes of global-scale travel, retail and food much more than as a response to issues of context and place.

As is evident from recent updates to Stansted Airport, these large projects must be designed to adapt to growth and development. In successive changes at Stansted, additional obstacles, layers and diversions have been required to allow for growing traveller numbers, changing retail patterns and increased security issues. As Chek Lap Kok aspires to welcome more flights than London's Heathrow Airport and New York's Kennedy Airport combined, it will be interesting to observe how the simplicity of the architect's concept is retained through change over time.

Discussion point:

[1] Urban infrastructure, such as airports, are often described as cities, but should they ever be designed as completed entities or should there be more open strategies that allow for flexibility and change?

Kevin Lynch describes points in the landscape as 'nodes'. He states that they are 'strategic points in the city, which are the intensive foci to and from which he is travelling'.[1] Within his explanation of the five elements that make up the city, the node is connected to the path, often acting as an intersection of two or more paths in the city. Lynch discusses the influence of such 'concentration nodes' over their surrounding districts.

→ ↓

Name: Ile de la Cité

Location: Paris, France

Date: 1852

Designer: Baron Georges-Eugène Haussmann

Case study: Haussmann Renovations

The changes made to Paris from 1852 until the end of the century transformed the French capital. What was built then, and is experienced to this day, was a collaboration between Napoléon III and the Seine Prefect that he appointed, Baron Georges-Eugène Haussmann. The Paris before this time was a web of narrow streets and cramped buildings, with poor sanitation and traffic congestion. This Paris had also been responsible for overthrowing several of Napoléon III's successors, and controlling the restless population was to be facilitated by a new approach to planning the city. Baron Haussmann was to lay out long wide boulevards through the city, destroying many of the old neighbourhoods and creating a network of spaces that would facilitate the movement of military troops. As in Cerdà's plan for Barcelona, new sewers were laid out and an emphasis on the city block set out regulations on building heights and the street wall. In the end, however, the authoritarian motives for these sweeping changes have been remembered more than any of the social benefits of the project.

Since 1852, these changes to Paris have provoked wide debate regarding the role of planning in social control and change. What is clear in the modernising work of Haussmann, is the impact of urban planning and design; these processes of development have an impact that reach beyond the building and the urban space to touch the economic, social and living conditions of everyone who lives in the city.

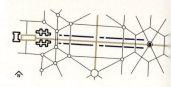

Discussion points:

[1] Should urban design and landscape architecture be considered neutral design processes?

[2] Who should the space be designed for? Who owns the space? Who will maintain the space? And who will have a right to use these spaces in the city?

1. Lynch, Kevin. *The Image of the City*. MIT Press, Cambridge and London, 1960. p. 48.

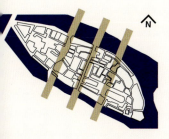

Case study: New Delhi

Half a century after the renovations of Paris began, the British Indian government marked the move of the national capital, from Calcutta to Delhi, with the design of a new city plan. Designed by Edwin Lutyens and completed in 1931, the city of New Delhi was located southwest of the original settlement and laid out in what Spiro Kostof calls 'the Grand Manner'.[2] This approach to designing cities was neither 'practical nor modest'; it conceived the city as a diagram of vistas, avenues and structures, behind which stands a powerful authority or government. These sentiments draw parallels with the Paris of Haussmann and Napoléon III. However, New Delhi was different in that it reached out beyond the existing city to engage with history and topography. Lutyens's design placed the Government House on the dominant Raisina Hill looking east towards Indraprastha, drawing a relationship between the ruling British government and the ancient settlements of India. While the combining of the two cultures is often complimented in the architectural critique of New Delhi, the urban plan is frequently criticised for representing a dominance over the people and the landscape of British-ruled India.

Kostof describes a 'propinquity between landscape design and urban design' in the cities of the Grand Manner.[3] The cities, such as New Delhi, Paris and Washington DC, used avenues and parks to fuse the city with the landscape, creating what was described as the 'City Beautiful Movement'. Rather than having the park as an escape from the city, as seen in Manhattan's Central Park, the City Beautiful and the later Garden City merged these formerly garden elements to create a new identity for the city.

Discussion point:

[1] How should we define the landscape? Is it the spaces between the buildings? Is it the green spaces of parks and gardens? Or is the whole city actually a landscape that needs to be considered as a connected system?

← ↑
....
Name: New Delhi

Location: Delhi, India

Date: 1931

Designer: Edwin Lutyens

2. Kostof, Spiro. *The City Shaped: The Elements of Urban Form Through History.* Thames and Hudson, London, 1992. p. 209.

3. *Ibid.* p. 226.

Case study: Lower Don Lands

The Lower Don Lands project was the result of an international design competition sponsored by the Toronto Waterfront Revitalization Corporation in 2007. The project is located at the mouth of the Don River – a site that has previously been on the edge of planning efforts by the city. The proposal for the 300-acre site addressed issues of identity in a wide landscape dominated by flood protection and habitat restoration; in this context, the design promotes an integration of new development, transportation infrastructure and open space networks.

The proposal developed by Stoss, along with Brown and Storey Architects and ZAS Architects, provides a cultural expression of landscape-oriented urbanism. Renewing the river, to allow it to function both ecologically and hydrologically, provides a structure that informs the spaces and the neighbourhoods of the city.

Discussion points:

[1] If urban design projects are informed by the landscape, how do we identify the unique nature of the landscape?

[2] What components, processes or layers exist that make a particular landscape unique, and how can this be interpreted so that the city can generate new urban forms?

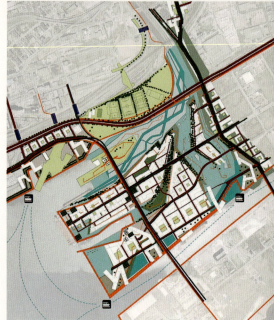

← ↙ ↓

Name: Lower Don Lands

Location: Toronto, Canada

Date: 2007

Designer: Stoss

Many urban design projects go unrealised. However, only a few of these set new paradigms for designing the city. Projects that go beyond what is possible to speculate on new urban futures are essential for both urban design and urban life. These concepts inform discussion, debate and new directions that provide a basis for future projects, some that may eventually be built.

Case study: Local Code

First published in 1993, the book *Local Code* is Michael Sorkin's written constitution for a city. Rather than using distinctive graphic representations to create the image of a possible city, the document uses specific code to explain in words what will make up this city and how it will operate. The *Local Code* begins with a Bill of Rights that states a citizen's right to pragmatic issues, such as safety and privacy, and more abstract statements, such as the private right to beauty. The coded manifesto goes on to outline principles for the city and its citizens, even stating measures of the physical conditions of the built environment.

Descriptions, percentages, distances and areas of measurement are used to specify the city's green and blue spaces, relationships to the territory, conditions of public space, composition of neighbourhoods, and the rules of city blocks. Without images to describe this speculation of a city, it is easy to imagine that this code could be applied anywhere. However, this is not a manifesto that could be applied to any city. It is the constitution of a city at 42°N latitude.

As with projects such as Frank Lloyd Wright's Broadacre City, the *Local Code* reaches beyond the built environment to address social, environmental, cultural and economic issues. Its classifications of Nabes, Habs and Tectons are reminiscent of Kevin Lynch's analysis of urban form in his book, *The Image of the City*; while its speculations of the life and form of the city reflect the research and ideas of LSE's Urban Age Project. The importance of projects such as these lies in their personal interpretations of reading and rewriting the city – and the belief that as urban designers, amazing futures can be planned and communicated in a multitude of media.

The map of Chicago (opposite), which sits at approximately 42°N latitude, demonstrates a carefully measured and varied block structure. While urban design plans are proposed through both drawn and written documents, accurate representation is essential to both media.

Discussion point:
[1] To speculate new forms for future cities, urban designers and landscape architects must understand and learn from the context of history. Will new designs be informed by previous theoretical and realised cities? Or will they mark a rupture with the past to set new directions?

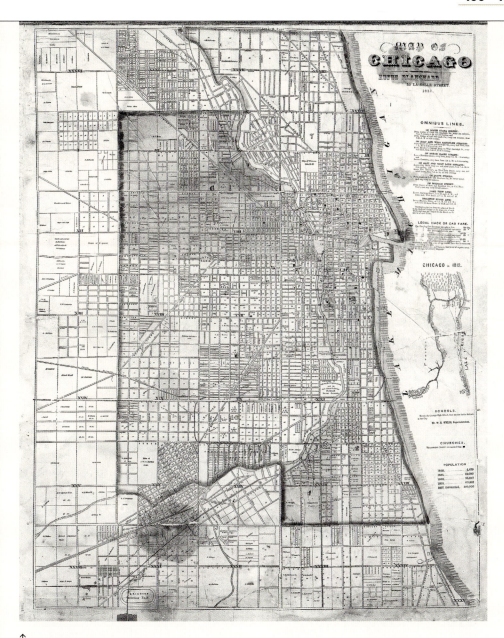

↑

Name: Map of Chicago

Location: Chicago, USA

Date: 1857

Designer: n/a

MAIN ACCESS POINTS AND PUBLIC SPACES

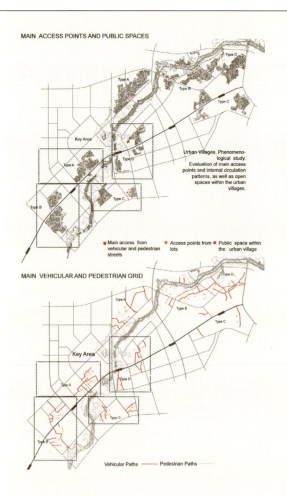

Urban Villages. Phenomeno-
logical study. Evaluation of main access
points and internal circulation
patterns, as well as open
spaces within the urban
villages.

● Main access from   ● Access points from   ● Public space within
vehicular and pedestrian   lots   the urban village
streets

MAIN VEHICULAR AND PEDESTRIAN GRID

Vehicular Paths — Pedestrian Paths

↖ ↑ →

Name: Deep Ground

Location: Longgang, China

Date: Ongoing

Designer: Groundlab

Projects and processes

Case study: Deep Ground

The Deep Ground project is the winning entry for a competition to design 11.8km² of urban fabric in the centre of Longgang. Situated in the Pearl River delta, northeast of Shenzhen, the design embraces the concept of 'thickened ground' to propose a 'surface that acquires thickness and spatial complexity as the different programs and land uses start to combine'.[1] This concept becomes evident in some specific areas of the plan and challenges the traditional premise of buildings versus landscape to realise surprisingly high densities with significant urban open spaces.

Like the Lower Don Lands project by Stoss, the Deep Ground proposal gives emphasis to the revitalisation of the river. This provides a new green infrastructure of biodiversity, connectivity and use around a strong infrastructural framework that is able to articulate the urban fabric and spaces in the city.

Groundlab has identified several existing villages within the site that they propose will provide a distinctiveness to the plan. These villages will contrast with the new structures that have been developed using parametric modelling. This process of relational urban modelling is based on urban relationships that connect with one another. Variables related to density and typology can be changed to generate and evaluate different models with relatively minor effort. While this approach has its critics, Groundlab's parametric model for Longgang has allowed for a more fluid design and decision-making process.

Discussion point:

[1] Schools of thought, such as landscape urbanism, can give a strong identity to new approaches in urban design – but how can we ensure that these ideas are more than just trends to re-package old ideas?

1. www.groundlab.org

Green is often used to represent physical landscape; here, it represents landscape as a process. These concluding projects all represent processes of the landscape that transform the city. Ecology, programme, development, sustainability and most importantly, processes of time and change, are crucial to each of these projects. They respond to the context and, in this process, they push back to influence the development of the city.

Case study: Xochimilco Ecological Park

Mario Schjetnan's approach for the design of the ecological park in Xochimilco has gained significant acclaim since its completion in 1993. The principles of ecological planning, which include environmental restoration, provision of open space and economic development, address many of the challenges of urbanisation in rapidly growing cities. What makes the work of Mario Schjetnan stand out from that of many other acclaimed landscape urbanists is his appreciation of local traditions, materials and aesthetics. Xochimilco Ecological Park responds to the history and the meaning of the landscape to reinterpret the floating islands that once filled much of the valley of Mexico.

Xochimilco means 'the place where flowers are grown'. The site dates back to before the Conquest, and possibly even before the Aztec era. It is a landscape of artificial garden islands called *chinampas*, constructed by piling soil on reed mats. These mats were anchored in place with willow trees. The site is a relic landscape of great age having been cultivated using engineered ecological processes that today would be considered cutting edge. The project cleanses contaminated surface water while the *chinampas* produce flowers and vegetables, and provide pasture for grazing. Gondolas and gondoliers also ply the canals and visitors can buy food from kitchen barges, while music from floating musicians drifts across the water.

Discussion point:
[1] Historical uses of the land are often used as conceptual drivers in both landscape architecture and urban design. How can the designer ensure that these have relevance to the future city as well as to the past?

↘ ↓ →
....
Name: Xochimilco Ecological Park

Location: Mexico City, Mexico

Date: 1993

Designer: Mario Schjetnan / Grupo de Diseño Urbano

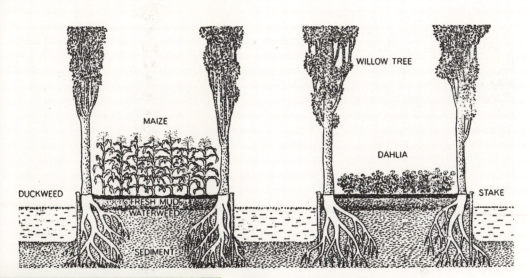

WILLOW TREE

MAIZE

DAHLIA

DUCKWEED

FRESH MUD
WATERWEED

STAKE

SEDIMENT

Case study: Governors Island

Located in the New York Harbor, 800m from Lower Manhattan, Governors Island has been strategic in the development of New York City. As a military and Coast Guard station for over 300 years, the island was significantly less developed than the rest of the city and therefore now offers the potential for future development led by an emphasis on large open spaces.

In 2007, West 8 was selected to design 90 acres of public space on this historic island. A large summer park is planned to stretch from Ligget Hall to the south tip of the island, while a Great Promenade will provide 360-degree access and views around the harbour. The urban design vision includes diverse ecological habitats, from striking hills to coastal marshes, free on-island bicycles, and unparalleled views of Manhattan, Brooklyn, and Staten Island and Liberty Island. Most importantly, the design promotes the public open space infrastructure ahead of any built development on the island. This sets a positive agenda for the importance of high-quality public amenities and creates a unique framework for attracting future development.

Discussion point:

[1] Parks can provide green infrastructure – a bold framework that can incorporate, accommodate or facilitate many urban systems and processes. Movement, recreation, water management and wildlife habitat are among these. How else can green infrastructure serve urban sustainability?

←↙↓

Name: Governors Island

Location: New York, USA

Date: 2007

Designer: West 8

Case study: Barcelona Forum

In 2004, the Barcelona Forum saw the completion of the Diagonal – first envisioned 150 years earlier by Ildefonso Cerdà. Where the avenue meets the sea, a new city district has been founded to reflect the sustainability principles of the Forum event. This truly mixed-use development has seen hotels, housing and public facilities juxtaposed with power generation, water treatment and waste management.

The design of the esplanade follows this approach to create a five-fingered blanket across the site. This acts as both a roof to many of the functional buildings and a framework for the arrangement of the utilities that weave through the floor. The esplanade appears as a five-coloured patchwork penetrated by structures and chimneys. The two most prominent structures are a pedestrian bridge that spans the marina to create new connections and a 4,500m² photovoltaic canopy that provides shelter from the summer sun and energy for local buildings. These urban forms provide a valuable infrastructure for a site that accommodates both fixed and ephemeral architecture, hopefully allowing it to evolve over time with increasing richness and diversity.

↑
Name: Barcelona Forum

Location: Barcelona, Spain

Date: 2004

Designer: Lapeña Torres

Discussion points:

[1] Is a city, as work of design, ever finished? What would it take to finish Barcelona?

[2] If cities are never finished, do they need to grow to survive? Or can they innovate and adapt in other ways to respond to changing demands?

Case study: Flowing Gardens

Flowing Gardens is a commission to design the site for the International Horticultural Fair in Xi'an. The design team, which includes Arup and Groundlab, proposes a plan of buildings, water, planting and circulation as a seamless system.

When the fair opens in 2011, the site will include an exhibition hall, a greenhouse and a gate building within the 37-hectare landscape. It is expected to receive 200,000 visitors a day. The buildings are described by the designers as an intensification of the natural ground conditions, allowing for the perception of a continuous landscape. The resulting plan shows a flowing circulation system that appears to mimic natural forms while influencing the appearance of the buildings.

Discussion points:

[1] If there is a line between landscape architecture and urban design, where is it? Is there a similar sort of line between architecture and urban design? Between planning and urban design?

[2] Is it important to establish boundaries between disciplines or do we all simply need to work better together?

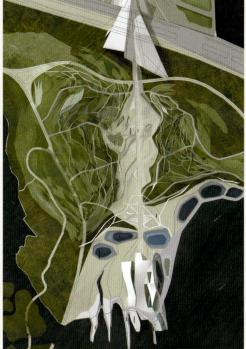

↑

Name: Flowing Gardens

Location: Xi'an, China

Date: Completion scheduled for 2011

Designer: Plasma Studio

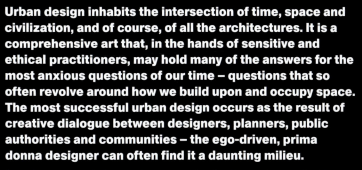

Urban design inhabits the intersection of time, space and civilization, and of course, of all the architectures. It is a comprehensive art that, in the hands of sensitive and ethical practitioners, may hold many of the answers for the most anxious questions of our time – questions that so often revolve around how we build upon and occupy space. The most successful urban design occurs as the result of creative dialogue between designers, planners, public authorities and communities – the ego-driven, prima donna designer can often find it a daunting milieu.

Landscape architects have particular importance to the work of urban design, bringing an understanding of urban landscapes as highly evolved ecological systems. In turn, landscape architects should aim to understand the wider urban structures that can inform their design of individual open spaces.

We have touched on the discourse between urban design and landscape architecture to identify the potential in well-designed cities and spaces. This book reveals some of this potential, but we have clearly omitted many other issues. What this book provides, however, is a framework of thoughts for the continued discourse and evolution of both landscape architecture and urban design.

←
....
Name: Mur Island

Location: Graz, Austria

Date: 2003

**Designer: Vito Acconci /
Acconci**

Vito Acconci's splendid design
for an artificial island in the Mur
River includes a café and a
small outdoor theatre. It shows
how it is sometimes possible for
a single, inspired and confident
move to refocus or reorientate
an entire city.

Access. 1. *n.* A point of entry to a site or building. 2. *v.* to approach or enter.

Architectures, the. *n.* A convenient term for all the professions and disciplines concerned with the three-dimensional design of buildings and/or landscapes. This includes, and is not limited to, building architecture, interior architecture, landscape architecture, landscape planning, urban design and urban planning.

Armature. *n.* 1. A framework that provides a supportive core for a sculpture, in particular, clay or papier-mâché sculpture. 2. The framework of urban space provided by building masses and the space between. 3. A polar arrangement in which urban space is arranged on an axis between two key attractors, as the poles on a magnet.

Axis. *n.* A central spine along which a site or building design is organised. Elements to either side of the axis may or may not be symmetrical.

Brief. *n.* An initial description of a project problem that defines the parameters within which the designer will work.

Building line. *n.* The line formed by the frontages of buildings along a street.

Built environment. *n.* The landscape where it has specifically been shaped by human design or influence.

CAD. *abbrev.* for: Computer Aided Design. Various software programs used as an aid to visualisation, presentation or construction drawings.

CHP. *abbrev.* for: Combined Heat and Power. A distributed system of localised heat and power generation that allows communities energy independence and self-sufficiency.

Circulation. *n.* The movement of people and vehicles through and around a site.

City block. *n.* 1. A usually rectangular unit of urban space bounded on all sides by streets, including the buildings within. 2. The measure of the length of one side of a regular, consecutive sequence of blocks as in, 'The shop is two blocks away'.

Code (*or* Design code). *n.* An often contractually binding document that outlines principles and measurements for the design of a new development. May sometimes also be applied to design regulations for conservation (*see* Design guidelines).

Community. 1. *n.* A group of people with interests in common. 2. An inhabited area populated with people who have interests in common, at least in part because of geographic proximity to each other (propinquity).

Composition. *n.* The arrangement of design elements in relation to each other, resulting in a pleasing unity.

Concept. *n.* An idea or abstract notion that serves to underpin a design proposal.

Context. *n.* The setting, circumstance, environment, and/or meaning of a defined site.

Contour. *n.* An imaginary line traced upon the surface of the land at a single elevation, which may be represented on a plan. Groupings of contours on a plan are used to indicate topography (*see* Topography).

Cultural landscape. *n.* A landscape that has developed in a distinctive way over time due to human occupation and influence.

Defensible space. *n.* A residential area that empowers its inhabitants, through the design of its buildings and external spaces, to take measures to ensure their own security.

Density. *n.* The number of people inhabiting an urban area. Usually measured in population/hectare.

Design guidelines. *n.* A usually discretionary document that outlines principles and measurements for the design of a new development. May sometimes also be applied to design regulations for conservation (*see* Code).

Ecology. *n.* The study of relationships between organisms and the environment, and of natural systems.

Elevation. *n.* 1. The distance of a specific point on the land above or below either sea level or a fixed reference point. 2. The facade of a building.

Environment. *n.* 1. A setting or milieu for something or someone. 2. The overall systems of land, water, vegetation, wildlife, etc that comprise the setting for life on earth.

FAR. *abbrev.* for: floor area ratio; it is the total building area divided by the site area. The use of FAR ratios allow the architect to choose between low-rise buildings that cover a greater area of the site or taller buildings that have a smaller footprint.

Figure/ground. *n.* A plan used for analysis that shows the relationship between built form and surrounding space. Generally, buildings are shown as black masses, or 'figures', on a white 'ground'. If the figure/ground drawing is showing open public space, then the ground may extend into public buildings.

Garden city. *n.* A low-density ex- or suburban town that seeks to provide the benefits of both town and country without the concomitant drawbacks.

Genius loci. *n.* Translates as 'the genius of the place'. The unique qualities of a place that should be taken into account and valued in a design for it.

GIS. *abbrev.* for: Geographic Information System. A computer system that allows for complex mapping, analysis, layering and comparison of geographic data.

Green infrastructure. *n.* The network of green spaces and water spaces required to support biodiversity, mitigate and adapt to climate change, and create salubrious human habitat within urban development.

Historic conservation. *n.* The work of designing for and protecting landscapes of historic and/or archaeological significance.

Human scale. *n.* The use of elements and massing within a site that relate well to humans and the way they use space.

Informal settlement. *n.* Housing assembled on land that has not been formally designated or serviced for residential use. Shanty towns and favelas are slum examples of informal settlement.

Infrastructure. *n.* The network of communications, transportation, and utility services required to support development (*see* Green infrastructure).

Landmark. *n.* A building, structure, sculpture or other landscape feature that stands out in a setting as a reference point.

Landscape urbanism. *n.* The theory of urbanism in which landscape is favoured over building architecture as the basic organising element for urban form.

Land use. *n.* The activity that takes place in a given area. Typical uses might include industry, housing, or playing fields. Rarely, however, is any landscape used for one activity alone.

Legibility. *n.* The ability of a place to be understood or navigated, often called 'reading the landscape'.

Massing. *n.* The three-dimensional relationship between the bulk of buildings in a grouping and landscape elements, such as trees and walls, and between buildings, landscape elements and their immediate landscape.

Masterplan. *n.* A plan or strategy for a complex development or environment, and the supporting documents that detail how the plan will be costed, built, administered and managed.

Measure. *n.* Dimensions, quantity or capacity as defined by an established, often legal, standard.

Microclimate. *n.* Average weather conditions in a small and specific area, such as the corner of a garden or the slope of a hill.

Mixed use. *n.* A variety of land uses within a building or in an area. A combination of housing, offices and shops in a neighbourhood is considered mixed use.

Modernism. *n.* A movement in arts and literature in the twentieth century that emphasised purity of form and emotion over ornamentation and sentimentality.

Movement. *n.* In urbanism, the often repetitive motion of people and transportation that shapes and is shaped by the form of urban spaces.

Natural surveillance. *n.* Often called 'eyes on the street', natural surveillance consists of maximising human presence and visibility to enhance public safety.

Neighbourhood. *n.* An area within a town or city that often has a distinct physical and social character.

New town. *n.* A development of housing, commerce, industry, transportation and all such elements of a standard town that is undertaken as a single, large-scale endeavour.

Node. *n.* A place where urban activities and circulation are concentrated.

Park. *n.* In urban terms, an often green and pleasantly landscaped area of land set aside for public use, in particular sports, recreation and relaxation, and also valuable for its ecological functions.

Permeability. *n.* The degree to which an area has routes through it.

Place. *n.* A space within the landscape that has acquired human meaning through human inhabitation.

Public realm. *n.* Any landscape area or building interior that is free for the use of all people at all times. Usually used in an urban context.

Public space. *n.* Any landscape area or building interior that is free for the use of all people at all times.

Representation. *n.* An image that stands for or symbolises an idea, concept or elements of the physical world.

Scale. *n.* 1. A standard proportion of measure that relates the dimensions of a representation to that which is represented. 2. The size or scope of an area or an issue, usually proportionally related to others.

Shared space. *n.* The theory and practice of removing the traditional separations, such as kerbs, fencing, and painted lines, between motor vehicles and pedestrians to encourage mutual responsibility for enhanced safety.

Site. *n.* An area that has been marked out for human use or action.

Skyscraper. *n.* There is no official height or number of storeys that identifies a building as a skyscraper, but it is generally a very tall building, the inhabitation of which would not be possible without mechanical lifts.

Street. *n.* A public way in a city or town, usually with sidewalks and flanked with houses or other buildings. The word also has a social sense that includes the living, working, gathering and interacting that occurs in the space of the street.

Suburb. *n.* A low-density residential area outlying a city, usually socially and economically dependent upon a relationship with that city, but often well serviced with shops and other facilities and amenities.

SuDS. *abbrev.* for: Sustainable Drainage Systems (formerly SUDS, abbrev. for Sustainable Urban Drainage Systems).

Sustainability. *n.* The doctrine of ensuring that the design, construction and occupation of a site are completely in balance with its total context, including the environment, sociological, cultural and economic considerations. Self-sufficiency, both individual and community, is usually at the heart of sustainability.

Territory. *n.* Traditionally, the land outlying a city that provided important resources, particularly food, through agriculture, hunting and fishing. Today the territory of a city is generally part of a dispersed global network that services numerous cities rather than an easily defined region around an urban core.

Topography. *n.* 1. The rise and fall of land and the natural and artificial features created by soil, rocks and buildings. In a more traditional sense, it also refers to the shape of the land created by the type of vegetation on the land. 2. The shape of the land and how it is described on maps or plans with contour lines.

Urban density. *n.* The interdisciplinary and collaborative work of shaping the three-dimensional spaces of human settlements with the intention to improve not just the beauty of a place, but to allow better interaction between people, and between people and their environment.

Urbanism. *n.* The study of cities, usually as a holistic discipline. Urbanism includes consideration of ecological, environmental, geographic, economic, political, social and cultural forces and their influence upon, and interrelationship with, the built environment.

Volume. *n.* Individual landscape spaces, like vessels, have volume. This volume is defined and contained by the planes of space – the ground plane, the overhead plane, and the vertical plane.

Watershed. *n.* A whole region that drains into a river or body of water.

Augé, Marc. **Non-places: Introduction to an Anthropology of Supermodernity**. Verso, London, 1995.

Bacon, Edmund N. **Design of Cities**, revised edition. Thames and Hudson, London, 1975.

Berman, Marshall. **All That Is Solid Melts into Air.** Penguin, 1988.

Carmona, Matthew; Heath, Tim; Oc, Taner; and Tiesdell, Steve. **Public Places – Urban Spaces: The Dimensions of Urban Design**. Architectural Press, Oxford, 2003.

Christopher, A.J. **The Atlas of Changing South Africa.** Routledge, London, 1994.

Cooper Marcus, Clare and Francis, Carolyn. **People Places: Design Guidelines for Urban Open Space,** Second Edition. Van Nostrand Reinhold, New York, 1998.

Corner, James, *Ed.* **Recovering Landscape: Essays in Contemporary Landscape Theory**. Princeton Architectural Press, New York, 2000.

Cowan, Robert. **The Dictionary of Urbanism**. Streetwise Press, Tisbury, Wiltshire, 2005.

Cullen, Gordon. **The Concise Townscape**. The Architectural Press, Oxford, 1961, 1971.

Gehl, Jan and Gemzøe, Lars. **New City Spaces**. The Danish Architectural Press, Copenhagen, 2003.

Gehl, Jan. **Life Between Buildings**. The Danish Architectural Press, Copenhagen, 1971.

Glancey, Jonathan. **Twentieth Century Architecture**. Carlton, London, 1998.

Hough, Michael. **Cities and Natural Process**. Routledge, London and New York, 1995.

Jacobs, Jane. **The Death and Life of Great American Cities**. Vintage Books, 1961.

Jellicoe, Geoffrey and Susan. **The Landscape of Man: Shaping the Environment from Prehistory to the Present Day**, Third Edition. Thames & Hudson, London, 1995.

Kostof, Spiro. **The City Assembled**. Thames & Hudson, London, 1999.

Kostof, Spiro. **The City Shaped**. Thames & Hudson, London, 1999.

LeGates, Richard T. and Stout, Frederic, Eds. **The City Reader**, second edition. Routledge, London and New York, 2000.

Llewelyn-Davies and Alan Baxter Associates. **Urban Design Compendium**. English Partnerships and The Housing Corporation, 2008.

Low, Setha and Smith, Neil. **The Politics of Public Space**. Routledge, New York 2006.

Lynch, Kevin. **The Image of the City**. MIT Press, Cambridge, Massachusetts, 1960.

Madanipour, Ali. **Design of Urban Space**. John Wiley and Sons, London, 1996.

Miles, Malcolm; Hall, Tim and Borden, Iain. **The City Cultures Reader**. Routledge, London and New York, 2000.

Reed, Peter. **Groundswell: Constructing the Contemporary Landscape**. Museum of Modern Art, New York, 2005.

Schroder, Thies. **Changes in Scenery: Contemporary Landscape Architecture in Europe**. Birkhauser, Basel, 2001.

Shane, David Grahame. **Recombinant Urbanism: Conceptual Modeling in Architecture, Urban Design and City Theory**. John Wiley and Sons, New York, 2005.

Simonds, John Ormsbee. **Landscape Architecture: A Manual of Site Planning and Design**. McGraw-Hill, New York, 1997.

Sorkin, Michael. **Some Assembly Required**. University of Minnesota Press, Minneapolis, 2001.

Sorkin, Michael. **Local Code**. Princeton Architectural Press, New York. 1993.

Spirn, Anne Whiston. **The Granite Garden: Urban Nature and Human Design**. Basic Books, New York, 1984.

Thompson, J. William and Sorvig, Kim. **Sustainable Landscape Construction**. Island Press, Washington, DC, 2000.

Tuan, Yi-Fu. **Space and Place: The Perspective of Experience**. University of Minnesota Press, Minneapolis, 1977.

Tung, Anthony M. **Preserving the World's Great Cities: The Destruction and Renewal of the Historic Metropolis**. Three Rivers Press, New York, 2001.

Venturi, R.; Brown, D. S.; and Izenour, S. **Learning from Las Vegas**. MIT Press, 1977.

Waldheim, Charles, *Ed.* **The Landscape Urbanism Reader**. Princeton Architectural Press, New York, 2006.

Whyte, William H. **The Social Life of Small Urban Spaces**. Project for Public Spaces Inc, 1980.

Worpole, Ken. **Here Comes the Sun: Architecture and Public Space in Twentieth-Century European Culture**. Reaktion Books, London, 2000.

Zapatka, Christian. **The American Landscape**. Princeton Architectural Press, New York, 1995.

Contacts and useful resources

Web resources

These websites provide excellent basic or general information to those who are interested to learn more about landscape architecture and urban design. Each also provides excellent links to other resources. For an extended list of European and international organisations in landscape architecture, please see *Fundamentals of Landscape Architecture*, also published by AVA Publishing in 2009.

Center for Livable Communities of the Local Government Commission
www.lgc.org/center

Centre de Cultura Contemporània Barcelona
www.urban.cccb.org

Council for European Urbanism
www.ceunet.org

CUBE: Centre for the Urban Built Environment
www.cube.org.uk

Design Trust for Public Space
www.designtrust.org

Greenbelt Alliance
www.greenbelt.org

Institute for Urban Design
www.instituteforurbandesign.org

International Council on Monuments and Sites (ICOMOS)
www.icomos.org

International Downtown Association
www.ida-downtown.org

International Federation of Landscape Architects (IFLA)
www.iflaonline.org

International Society of City and Regional Planners (ISOCARP)
www.isocarp.org

I Want to Be a Landscape Architect
www.iwanttobealandscapearchitect.com

Land8Lounge
www.land8lounge.com

LarcExchange
www.larcexchange.com

Metropolis
www.metropolis.org

National Trust for Historic Preservation
www.preservationnation.org

Project for Public Spaces
www.pps.org

Resource for Urban Design Information (RUDI)
www.rudi.net

The Forum for Urban Design
www.forumforurbandesign.org

UN Habitat United Nations Human Settlement Program
www.unhabitat.org

Urban Design Group
www.udg.org.uk

Urban Ecology
www.urbanecology.org

Urban Land Institute
www.uli.org

Van Alen Institute
www.vanalen.org

Professional journals

The breadth of the fields of landscape and urbanism means that there are thousands of journals that are pertinent to different areas. The list below is a selection:

a+u Architecture and Urbanism (Japan)
www.japan-architect.co.jp

ARQ Chile
**www.scielo.cl/scielo.php?script=sci_serial&
pid=0717-6996**

Arquitetura & Urbanismo (Brazil)
www.revistau.com.br

Garten + Landschaft (Germany)
www.garten-landschaft.de

Green Places
www.landscape.co.uk/greenplaces/journal

Harvard Design Magazine
**www.gsd.harvard.edu/research/publications/
hdm**

IFLA Online Journal
www.iflajournal.org

Jornal da Paisagem (Brazil)
www.jornaldapaisagem.unisul.br

Journal of Urban Design
www.tandf.co.uk/journals/titles/13574809.asp

Journal of Urbanism
www.tandf.co.uk/journals/titles/17549175.asp

Kerb: The Journal of Landscape Architecture
www.kerbjournal.com

Landscape (UK)
www.wardour.co.uk

Landscape Architecture Australia
www.aila.org.au/landscapeaustralia

Landscape Architecture New Zealand
www.agm.co.nz

Landscape Journal
**www.wisc.edu/wisconsinpress/journals/journ
als/lj.html**

Landscape Management
www.landscapemanagement.net

Landscape Research
**www.tandf.co.uk/journals/carfax/01426397.ht
ml**

Landscapes/Paysages (Canada)
www.csla.ca

Landskab (Denmark)
www.arkfo.dk

Metropolis
www.metropolismag.com

New Urban News
www.newurbannews.com

Places Journal
www.places-journal.org

Regeneration and Renewal
www.regen.net

Sustainable Land Development Today
www.sldtonline.com

Terrain.org A Journal of Built and Natural Environments
www.terrain.org

Topos: The International Review of Landscape Architecture and Urban Design
www.topos.de

Urban Design Journal
www.udg.org.uk/?section_id=61

Urban Green File (South Africa)
www.brookepattrick.co.za

Acknowledgements

We would like to express our sincere gratitude to our families for their support, in particular our partners, Jason and Kristin.

We are indebted to our friends, colleagues and collaborators for their great advice and for the stunning images included in the book. We would also like to mention the institutions for whom we work, which help us put food on the table and continue to feed our heads with ideas. Ed Wall lectures at Kingston University and Tim Waterman at the Writtle School of Design.

The Landscape Institute has been a tremendous support, in particular Paul Lincoln and, in the library and archive, Lesley Malone and Annabel Downs.

At AVA publishing, we are grateful to Renée Last for her conscientious editing and for extending deadlines again and again. Leonie Taylor helped source all the imagery for the book, and the book was designed David Smith.

Pages 104–105: Courtesy of Dixon Jones Ltd.
Pages 106–107: Courtesy of VMX Architects.
Page 108: Courtesy of Building Design Partnership.
Page 109: © www.Shutterstock.com/Losevsky Pavel.
Page 110: Mobius Bench image courtesy of Acconci Studio.
Pages 110–111: © www.Shutterstock.com/Ewa Walicka/Hsinli Wang.
Page 112: © The Lowry Collection, Salford.
Pages 116–117: Courtesy of Rogers, Stirk, Harbour and Partners.
Pages 120–121: Alphaville image © Free Agents Limited/CORBIS. *Hollow Land* illustration by Eyal Weizman, 2004.
Page 123: Courtesy of Bo01 Malmo.
Page 125: Photos supplied by Tim Waterman.
Page 126: Courtesy of Farrer Huxley Associates.
Page 127: Courtesy of Venturi, Scott Brown and Associates.
Pages 128–129: © www.Shutterstock.com/Jeremy Reddington.
Page 131: Liberia image © www.iStock.com/Ines Gesell. Elephant and Castle image supplied by Ed Wall.
Pages 132–133: Boston image © www.iStock.com/Jorge Salcedo. Millenium Dome image © iStock.com/Christopher Steer. PS1 image supplied by Ed Wall.
Pages 134–135: Images © www.Shutterstock.com/Ryby/Alberto Perez Viega. Southbank Centre image supplied by Ed Wall.
Pages 136, 140–141: Photographs by Camlin Lonsdale / Drawings by Camlin Lonsdale.
Page 143: Diagram supplied by Ed Wall. © www.Shutterstock.com/Zina Seletskaya.

Page 145: Photos and diagram Ed Wall.
Pages 150–151: Chek Lap Kok images courtesy of Foster and Partners. Euralille images courtesy of The Office for Metropolitan Architecture.
Pages 152–153: Paris and New Delhi images © www.Shutterstock.com/Demid/Jeremy Richards. Diagrams supplied by Ed Wall.
Pages 154–155: Courtesy of Stoss.
Page 156: Courtesy of The Chicago History Museum.
Pages 158–159: All rights reserved Groundlab Ltd.
Pages 160–161: Courtesy of Mario Schjetnan / Grupo Diseño Urbano. Drawing by Robert Coe. Photographs by Jean-Gerard Sidaner, Gabriel Figueroa and Michael Calderwood.
Page 164: Images supplied by the authors.
Page 165: © Plasma Studio.
Page 166: Courtesy of Acconci Studio.

Book design by David Smith, Atelier.

All reasonable attempts have been made to trace, clear and credit the copyright holders of the images reproduced in this book. However, if any credits have been inadvertently omitted, the publisher will endeavour to incorporate amendments in future editions.

Publisher's note

The subject of ethics is not new, yet its consideration within the applied visual arts is perhaps not as prevalent as it might be. Our aim here is to help a new generation of students, educators and practitioners find a methodology for structuring their thoughts and reflections in this vital area.

AVA Publishing hopes that these **Working with ethics** pages provide a platform for consideration and a flexible method for incorporating ethical concerns in the work of educators, students and professionals. Our approach consists of four parts:

The **introduction** is intended to be an accessible snapshot of the ethical landscape, both in terms of historical development and current dominant themes.

The **framework** positions ethical consideration into four areas and poses questions about the practical implications that might occur. Marking your response to each of these questions on the scale shown will allow your reactions to be further explored by comparison.

The **case study** sets out a real project and then poses some ethical questions for further consideration. This is a focus point for a debate rather than a critical analysis so there are no predetermined right or wrong answers.

A selection of **further reading** for you to consider areas of particular interest in more detail.

Ethical: awareness/ reflection/ debate

Introduction

Ethics is a complex subject that interlaces the idea of responsibilities to society with a wide range of considerations relevant to the character and happiness of the individual. It concerns virtues of compassion, loyalty and strength, but also of confidence, imagination, humour and optimism. As introduced in ancient Greek philosophy, the fundamental ethical question is: *what should I do?* How we might pursue a 'good' life not only raises moral concerns about the effects of our actions on others, but also personal concerns about our own integrity.

In modern times the most important and controversial questions in ethics have been the moral ones. With growing populations and improvements in mobility and communications, it is not surprising that considerations about how to structure our lives together on the planet should come to the forefront. For visual artists and communicators, it should be no surprise that these considerations will enter into the creative process.

Some ethical considerations are already enshrined in government laws and regulations or in professional codes of conduct. For example, plagiarism and breaches of confidentiality can be punishable offences. Legislation in various nations makes it unlawful to exclude people with disabilities from accessing information or spaces. The trade of ivory as a material has been banned in many countries. In these cases, a clear line has been drawn under what is unacceptable.

But most ethical matters remain open to debate, among experts and lay-people alike, and in the end we have to make our own choices on the basis of our own guiding principles or values. Is it more ethical to work for a charity than for a commercial company? Is it unethical to create something that others find ugly or offensive?

Specific questions such as these may lead to other questions that are more abstract. For example, is it only effects on humans (and what they care about) that are important, or might effects on the natural world require attention too?

Is promoting ethical consequences justified even when it requires ethical sacrifices along the way? Must there be a single unifying theory of ethics (such as the Utilitarian thesis that the right course of action is always the one that leads to the greatest happiness of the greatest number), or might there always be many different ethical values that pull a person in various directions?

As we enter into ethical debate and engage with these dilemmas on a personal and professional level, we may change our views or change our view of others. The real test though is whether, as we reflect on these matters, we change the way we act as well as the way we think. Socrates, the 'father' of philosophy, proposed that people will naturally do 'good' if they know what is right. But this point might only lead us to yet another question: *how do we know what is right?*

You
What are your ethical beliefs?

Central to everything you do will be your attitude to people and issues around you. For some people, their ethics are an active part of the decisions they make every day as a consumer, a voter or a working professional. Others may think about ethics very little and yet this does not automatically make them unethical. Personal beliefs, lifestyle, politics, nationality, religion, gender, class or education can all influence your ethical viewpoint.

Using the scale, where would you place yourself? What do you take into account to make your decision? Compare results with your friends or colleagues.

Your client
What are your terms?

Working relationships are central to whether ethics can be embedded into a project, and your conduct on a day-to-day basis is a demonstration of your professional ethics. The decision with the biggest impact is whom you choose to work with in the first place. Cigarette companies or arms traders are often-cited examples when talking about where a line might be drawn, but rarely are real situations so extreme. At what point might you turn down a project on ethical grounds and how much does the reality of having to earn a living affect your ability to choose?

Using the scale, where would you place a project? How does this compare to your personal ethical level?

01 02 03 04 05 06 07 08 09 10   01 02 03 04 05 06 07 08 09 10

Your specifications
What are the impacts of your materials?

In relatively recent times, we are learning that many natural materials are in short supply. At the same time, we are increasingly aware that some man-made materials can have harmful, long-term effects on people or the planet. How much do you know about the materials that you use? Do you know where they come from, how far they travel and under what conditions they are obtained? When your creation is no longer needed, will it be easy and safe to recycle? Will it disappear without a trace? Are these considerations your responsibility or are they out of your hands?

Using the scale, mark how ethical your material choices are.

Your creation
What is the purpose of your work?

Between you, your colleagues and an agreed brief, what will your creation achieve? What purpose will it have in society and will it make a positive contribution? Should your work result in more than commercial success or industry awards? Might your creation help save lives, educate, protect or inspire? Form and function are two established aspects of judging a creation, but there is little consensus on the obligations of visual artists and communicators toward society, or the role they might have in solving social or environmental problems. If you want recognition for being the creator, how responsible are you for what you create and where might that responsibility end?

Using the scale, mark how ethical the purpose of your work is.

01 02 03 04 05 06 07 08 09 10

01 02 03 04 05 06 07 08 09 10

Working with publicly owned spaces is an aspect of landscape architecture that involves the discipline with issues of politics, society and ethics. The creation or restoration of public parks and buildings, housing estates, city squares, infrastructure or coastlines is a multidisciplinary activity where decisions can have large-scale consequences. Projects often reflect social attitudes of the time towards nature, communities, integration and freedom of movement. The best interests of the public should ideally be maintained, but this might be difficult amongst conflicting pressures from financial interests or political reputations. Similarly, what might benefit the taxpayer may have an adverse impact on the natural environment. Having a clear ethical stance or code of conduct from the outset can be crucial to negotiating such conflicts with any conviction. Consulting with the public or directly involving them with the design process is one possible route to pursuing a more inclusive, diverse and ethical approach to creating public spaces, but at the same time this might adversely create feelings of animosity or be accused of being an act of tokenism that only incurs the need for more time and money.

Landscape architect Andrew Jackson Downing first voiced and publicised the need for New York's Central Park in 1844. Supporters were primarily the wealthy, who admired the public grounds of London and Paris, and argued that New York needed a similar facility to establish its international reputation. The State appointed a Central Park Commission to oversee the development and in 1857, a landscape design contest was held. Writer Frederick Law Olmsted and English architect Calvert Vaux developed the Greensward Plan, which was selected as the winning design.

Before construction could start, the designated area had to be cleared of its inhabitants, most of whom were poor and either African Americans or immigrants. Roughly 1600 people were evicted under the rule of 'eminent domain', which allowed the government to seize private property for public purposes.

Following the completion of the park in 1873 it quickly slipped into decline, largely due to lack of interest from the New York authorities. Times were also changing; cars had been invented and were becoming commonplace. No longer were parks to be used only for walks and picnics, but people now wanted spaces for sports.

In 1934, Fiorello LaGuardia was elected mayor of New York City and gave Robert Moses the job of cleaning up Central Park. Lawns and trees were replanted, walls were sandblasted, bridges were repaired and major redesigning and construction work was carried out (19 playgrounds and 12 ball fields were created). By the 1970s, Central Park had become a venue for public events on an unprecedented scale, including political rallies and demonstrations, festivals and massive concerts. But at the same time, the city of New York was in economic and social crisis. Morale was low and crime was high. Central Park saw an era of vandalism, territorial use and illicit activity. As a result, several citizen groups emerged to reclaim the park and called for proper planning and management.

The outcome was the establishment of the office of Central Park Administrator and the Central Park Conservancy was subsequently founded. Central Park was redesigned with a revolutionary zone-management system. Every zone has a specific individual accountable for its day-to-day maintenance. As of 2007, the Conservancy had invested approximately US$450 million in restoration and management. Today, Central Park is the most visited park in the United States with around 25 million visitors annually.

What responsibility does a landscape architect have to ensure a public space is maintained once it is complete?

Was it unethical to evict people in order to build a public park? Would this happen today?

Would you have worked on this project?

Commissioned by clients to install barrier walls and private pathways that can keep out or discourage those who are unwanted, or hired to create private commercial experiences out of what may have been public space, many become complicit in structuring the urban language of separation.

Ellen Posner
(former architecture critic)
'Cities for a Small Planet'
The Wall Street Journal

Further reading

AIGA
Design business and ethics
2007, AIGA

Eaton, Marcia Muelder
Aesthetics and the good life
1989, Associated University Press

Ellison, David
Ethics and aesthetics in European modernist literature:
from the sublime to the uncanny
2001, Cambridge University Press

Fenner, David E W (Ed)
Ethics and the arts:
an anthology
1995, Garland Reference Library of Social Science

Gini, Al and Marcoux, Alexei M
Case studies in business ethics
2005, Prentice Hall

McDonough, William and Braungart, Michael
Cradle to cradle:
remaking the way we make things
2002, North Point Press

Papanek, Victor
Design for the real world:
making to measure
1972, Thames and Hudson

United Nations Global Compact
The ten principles
www.unglobalcompact.org/AboutTheGC/TheTenPrinciples/index.html